DUCT TAPE KILLER

THE TRUE INSIDE STORY OF SEXUAL SADIST & MURDERER
ROBERT LEROY ANDERSON

from the authors of the bestselling true-crime memoir *Gitchie Girl*
PHIL HAMMAN & SANDY HAMMAN
with Former Attorney General LARRY LONG

ELECTIO PUBLISHING
first century principles.
a twenty-first century approach.

Duct Tape Killer: The True Inside Story of Sexual Sadist & Murderer Robert Leroy Anderson
By Phil Hamman & Sandy Hamman

Copyright 2020 by Phil Hamman & Sandy Hamman
Cover Design by eLectio Publishing

ISBN-13: 978-1-63213-706-7
Published by eLectio Publishing, LLC
Little Elm, Texas
http://www.eLectioPublishing.com

Printed in the United States of America

5 4 3 2 1 eLP 25 24 23 22 21 20

The eLectio Publishing editing team is comprised of: Christine LePorte, Lori Draft, Sheldon James, Court Dudek, and Jim Eccles.

Publisher's Note
The publisher does not have any control over and does not assume any responsibility for author or third-party websites or their content.

From the beginning of mankind,
there has been a raging battle
between good and evil
for control of the world.

This book is dedicated
to moral people.

In the end,
good shall prevail.

Note to the Reader

Duct Tape Killer is not always told in chronological order but rather alternates from the crimes to the investigation. The story that follows is true, and every effort was made to recreate situations exactly as they occurred. The names are real; no pseudonyms are used. The information and dialogue come from investigative reports, court documents, evidence, written records, and live interviews with people who were involved in this heartrending story. The official paperwork provided for our research was very detailed and organized.

Contents

Acknowledgments

It takes a team effort to write a book like *Duct Tape Killer* as the information is garnered from a variety of sources. We express gratitude to the many newspaper journalists and their thorough articles related to these crimes. The personnel working in court and police records helped gather important documents. To those people who graciously gave us their time for interviews, especially retired Sheriff Gene Taylor, his wife, Lois, and former DCI agents Bob Grandpre and Jim Severson, we express a heartfelt thank-you.

A special thanks to Cory Meyers, news director, and the entire staff at the Sioux Falls *Argus Leader*. You demonstrated professionalism, patience throughout lengthy proceedings, and skill in covering a case that was stressful and demanding. Your coverage of the crimes helped us to organize and confirm facts.

It was important to get an accurate portrayal of how the prison operated and appeared in the 1990s. Communications and Information Manager Michael Winder provided information regarding the ad seg wing of the state penitentiary. For this, we are grateful.

To Amy Schmidt, we appreciate your editing advice. Also, thanks to everyone at eLectio Publishing as your never-failing support and hard work continue to convey success.

—Phil and Sandy Hamman

It took nearly five years of dedicated and cooperative efforts by several law enforcement agencies to achieve the end results in these cases. The McCook County Sheriff's Office, Minnehaha County Sheriff's Office, Lincoln County Sheriff's Office, Tea Police Department, Sioux Falls Police Department, South Dakota Department of Corrections, South Dakota Department of Game, Fish, and Parks, South Dakota National Guard, South Dakota Division of Criminal Investigation, South Dakota Highway Patrol, and the state crime lab were each instrumental in this process. Monstrous crimes were committed upon Larisa Dumansky and Piper Streyle and attempted on Amy Anderson and several others. All of these crimes might have gone unsolved without the diligent work of the agencies listed above. This chronicle could be written only because of your efforts. Thank you to each.

Those of us who worked on these cases were grateful for the unprecedented assistance from dozens of ordinary citizens. Their willingness to come forward with information provided several items of important evidence. Some of these individuals are named in this book; others are not. Named or unnamed, thank you for your help.

The prosecution team was comprised of South Dakota Attorney General Mark Barnett, McCook County State's Attorney Roger Gerlach, Assistant Attorney General Patty Froning (now Devaney), and me. Each of us was responsible for a portion of the work, but the division of labor was not equal. Patty carried the heaviest load, and the volume and quality of her work were unsurpassed. We are all indebted to her.

These cases generated thousands of pages of police reports, transcripts, legal documents, and evidence. The prosecution team relied almost exclusively on Jeannette Pfeiffer, my legal assistant at the attorney general's office, to maintain control of all this data. She is one of the most organized people I have ever known. Thank you, Jeannette.

I worked on these cases from the fall of 1996 through the spring of 1999. The first trial in Aberdeen lasted four weeks. The second trial in Sioux Falls took three months. I was away from home a lot. My wife, Jan, and our children, Claire and Craig, patiently carried on in my absence, appreciating the importance of my responsibility. To Jan and Claire and Craig, thank you.

—Larry Long

Prologue

FEAR, ANXIETY, AND REVULSION gripped the region as word spread regarding women being abducted, one brazenly taken from her home in broad daylight. The near kidnapping of another who had to fight for her life on a dark, secluded highway escalated the fear. In the tranquil area of southeast South Dakota where family and religious values flourished, the news was perceived as unreal. When an elite team of investigators cracked the case and details were released to the public, the lives of these women took on a personal feel to the residents of their communities.

The deranged mind of Robert Leroy Anderson, a sexual sadist, rapist, and murderer, came to light. We had the privilege of meeting former attorney general, judge, and prosecutor Larry Long. Despite the intense heat of late summer, he wore a long-sleeved white button-up shirt, a whimsical purple paisley tie, and polished black wingtips. He emanated sophistication, and when he spoke, it was with refined wisdom. We sat with objective fascination as Mr. Long shared information about the case with the use of over one hundred photos. We discussed the possibilities of writing a book and explained with honesty that we had been contacted by more than a dozen people wanting us to write a book about their life. In the end, we chose to work with Larry Long and write *Duct Tape Killer*. This tragic account also contains the glimmers of eternal hope and the stories of people who fought to overcome evil rather than succumb to it. *Duct Tape Killer* is the dark story of a demented man who stalked and planned appalling acts upon his victims. It also depicts the continued struggles good people face in a world filled with unspeakable evil.

—Phil & Sandy Hamman

Duct Tape Killer **alternates in chronological order.**
Below is a basic timeline laid out
in the sequence in which events occurred.

- Anderson plots. He begins to invent devices to help abduct women. Early 1990s.
- Glen Walker agrees to assist Anderson with the crimes. Spring 1994.
- Larisa Dumansky vanishes from the Morrell's parking lot. August 27, 1994.
- Amy Anderson (no relation) fights for her life on a secluded highway. November 10, 1994.
- Anderson exhumes Larisa's grave. July 25 and 26, 1996.
- Anderson is foiled in his attempt to abduct Piper Streyle. Friday, July 26, 1996.
- Anderson successfully kidnaps Piper. Monday, July 29, 1996.
- Investigators first interview Anderson. July 30, 1996.
- The first trial for kidnapping Piper begins. April 8, 1997.
- The shrewd inmate, Jeremy Brunner, cons Anderson. Late summer 1997.
- The murder trial begins. March 1999.

Serial killers make up only
0.00039% of the population.
The odds of being a victim
of this type of killer
are astronomically
low.

Be alert and of sober mind. Your enemy the devil prowls around like a roaring lion looking for someone to devour.

—1 Peter 5:8 (NIV)

The Phone Call
July 29, 1996

SOMETHING WAS WRONG. Twenty-seven-year-old Piper Streyle, dependable and responsible, had not shown up for work. As an employee of Southeastern Mental Health Outreach (SMHO), she provided home assistance to a mother and son, who were both disabled. She was punctual and efficient, so when 3:00 PM rolled around and Piper had not shown up, the mother called SMHO and talked to Piper's coworker, Patty Sinclair. Piper was an hour late. While Patty dialed Piper's number, she tried to push away a nagging concern; likely there was a miscommunication that would soon be cleared up. The phone rang repeatedly at the home Piper shared with her husband, Vance, and two young children. Shaina was three and a half and Nathan had turned two yesterday. Finally, Patty heard the distinct clatter of the receiver being lifted.

"Hello," Shaina said quietly.

"Is your mommy or daddy home?" Patty asked.

"No."

"Is there a babysitter?"

"No. They are killed. A mean man carried Mommy away."

Click.

Patty called back immediately, her pulse rising with each successive ring of the phone until finally a small voice answered. It was the little girl again, and now she was sobbing hysterically. Patty's gut instinct was to keep the little girl talking to calm her down.

"When did Mommy leave?"

"A while ago."

"Where did she go?"

"She went with a man in a black car."

"Do you know the man?"

"No. I don't want my mommy to die. I don't want Daddy hurt. I don't want Daddy to die."

Patty was able to get the attention of a coworker and directed her to call 911.

"Have Patty keep talking to the little girl, and we'll try to get more information," the 911 operator directed.

So, Patty asked the girl her name.

"Shaina," she sobbed. "My mommy is going to die." She hung up again.

Early 1990s (Ukraine) – August 1994 (USA)

A NEW LIFE. A better life. That was the dream of Bill and Larisa Dumansky. The Ukraine had become unstable as the country sought independence from Russia. Political strife created a terrible economic crisis, and a steady job was difficult to find. Adding to the pressure was the fact that the Dumansky family was Christian. Bill's father was a Pentecostal minister, a denomination banned by the government. To avoid the watchful eye of government officials, Christians held worship services at night in the forest or in secluded basements. Schoolteachers encouraged children to denounce God, and those who preached His word lived in constant fear of being arrested and sentenced to prison, tortured, or executed. Through the efforts of Lutheran Social Services, the Dumanskys qualified for asylum due to religious persecution and settled in Sioux Falls, South Dakota, where they joined his parents, brother, and five sisters.

This city nestled in the southeast corner of the state was the largest city in South Dakota, though it boasted a population of less than 100,000. The winding Big Sioux River with its cascading waterfalls along with pristine parks and pre-war Japanese gardens immediately felt like home to Bill and Larisa. The city would in fact become nationally ranked as the best city to live in the United States based on numerous factors, including health care, employment, home prices, and low crime rates. The citizens of the Midwestern town did not readily tolerate crime, and many neighborhoods worked with the police department to form watch groups.

When both Bill and Larisa landed good-paying jobs at the local John Morrell meatpacking plant, the couple knew they could provide a stable life for their two daughters, Kristina and Regina. The factory loomed over the north side of Sioux Falls like a brick and steel giant with towering smokestacks stretching into the sky. The plant skirted the lower-income housing areas that crept into the extreme northeast part known for its aging homes with front porches, family dogs roaming freely, and backyards dotted with yellow dandelions beneath clotheslines. The packing house ran shifts around the clock and processed beef, pork, and lamb to sell across the nation. It was a welcome job for many immigrants like Bill and Larisa who wanted to get a solid start. Gradually the couple began to get ahead financially. Bill left Morrell's and took a day shift laying carpet and flooring while Larisa continued working the night shift at the packing house from 4:00 PM to 1:00 AM. She would go home, shower, then slip into bed so as not to wake Bill. She would snuggle next to her husband, even more so as their love had deepened. Larisa was six weeks pregnant.

A Husband's Distress
July 29, 1996, late afternoon

MCCOOK COUNTY SHERIFF Gene Taylor was dispatched to the Streyle residence, a trailer house located west of Sioux Falls near Canistota. He was not informed about the conversation between the employees of SMHO and the 911 operator but was only told to check on the welfare of a child. The locals made frequent comparisons between their own Sheriff Taylor and television Sheriff Andy Taylor from *The Andy Griffith Show* due to his easygoing yet alert nature. In 1966 he was drafted for the Vietnam War. When his commander asked for volunteers to become military police, Taylor said, "I must have gotten my hand up faster than some of the others." He was one of the few chosen to be trained as an MP. He returned home and became sheriff a decade later, a title he would hold for 28 years.

Upon approaching the Streyle trailer, Taylor felt immediately unsettled. Three steps led to a large deck off the entrance to the trailer. He noted that the bottom board was knocked off, and the second step was broken, tilted at an awkward angle; for some reason it looked as though it had recently occurred. The front door hung open and a gaping hole stood where there should have been glass in the screen door. Taylor knocked and called out, "This is Sheriff Taylor. Is anyone home?" He called out several more times to no avail, although he heard young voices inside the home. Since he came to check on the welfare of children, he decided to enter the residence. He opened the door and immediately knew something was amiss.

The crowded living room, a testament to the many household items required when raising children, was clean but cluttered with a mass of toys and stuffed animals strewn liberally about the sofa, floor, and upright piano. A chair and ironing board, among other items, were tipped over or in disarray. A steak knife protruded from a wastebasket near the front door. *It looks like there was a struggle and that someone left in a hurry.* A woman's purse lay surrounded by a checkbook, calculator, and bills. He called out again, but there was still no answer.

Taylor entered the hallway and spotted a small girl, who burst into tears. He bent down to look her in the eyes.

"Do you know where your mom is?"

"My mommy is going to die!"

"Is your mom in the hospital?"

"No." The girl hugged herself and cried uncontrollably. Taylor heard a small noise in one of the bedrooms, and a boy, hardly more than a toddler, came running to his sister's side. Taylor asked a few more questions which only caused her to cry harder.

He immediately called for backup, and a horde of authorities converged on the scene including Division of Criminal Investigation agent Jim Severson. He knelt on one knee and had Shaina sit on the other knee. He gently began asking her what happened.

She continued crying and squeezed her hands together nervously. "A bad man in a black truck came. There was a loud noise, and Mommy said to get Nathan and hide."

Shaina's answers were interrupted by the ringing of the phone in another room. Taylor picked up the receiver.

"Hello."

"Who is this?" the voice on the other end demanded.

"This is McCook County Sheriff Gene Taylor. Who is this?"

"Vance Streyle. I'm looking for my kids. Is something wrong?" Unable to make contact with his wife around noon, Vance assumed the children would be at the babysitter's house and went there.

"Your kids are safe, but I need you to come home as soon as possible."

Vanished
August 27, 1994

THE CONTINUED BUZZING of the alarm clock brought Bill Dumansky out of a deep sleep. His wife, Larisa, always turned it off, but today the piercing noise continued. Morning sunrays shimmered through the curtains, causing him to stir and open his eyes. He rolled onto his side, but something wasn't right. Larisa was not in bed. Thinking she got up for some reason, he walked through the house, but his wife was nowhere, and her minivan was not in the driveway. Bill threw on some clothes and made a few phone calls to friends and coworkers, who also had not seen Larisa. His concern turned to anxiety, and he phoned two hospital emergency rooms to see if something might have happened. Then he decided to drive around in hopes of locating his wife. She had definitely arrived at work by 4:00 PM the previous day, since she called Bill during her break. She was happy and in a playful mood. They were having guests the next day and discussed the menu. By 7:30 AM he was driving through the employee parking lot scanning the stretching rows of vehicles until finally he spotted her minivan just ahead and let out a small sigh of relief. He parked behind the van, but his stomach clenched at the first thing he noticed. The front driver's side tire was completely flat, and even more disturbing were the van keys dangling from the driver's side door lock. Bill rushed to a telephone and called the police.

Although the detectives were concerned, they also operated from the standpoint of realizing that she could be with a friend or relative.

In 99% of cases nationwide, the missing person is located within 24 hours. Lieutenant Gary Folkerts explained this fact to Bill. But because of the unusual circumstances, including the flat tire and key left in the door, the detectives soon opened a missing person's case. They dusted the minivan for fingerprints and checked other forensic details, but it showed nothing of value. When asked about the flat tire, Bill explained that she had recurring flat tires in the last two months, most which happened in the Morrell's parking lot. Twice her tires were punctured. Bill claimed to have checked the tires himself and found a cut in the valve stem of the tire which caused a slow leak. The explanation was unconvincing, and Bill became a primary suspect.

Another suspicious situation arose. Knowing how difficult it was to be an immigrant in a new country, Larisa was helping a Russian coworker who lost his driver's license for operating a vehicle while intoxicated. He was on work release from the county jail for a couple of months, and Larisa gave him a ride back to the jail each night since they worked the same hours. An agent immediately began checking out the man's story.

There were thousands of other leads as well. Morrell's employed 3,600 people who might know something. However, the field was narrowed to 100 people most likely to have had contact with Larisa. Knowing that a perpetrator could be orbiting around her workplace, six FBI agents were brought in to help with the interviews, but none of them yielded anything of value. It felt as if they were cornering smoke. Each promising lead that surfaced turned to disappointment, including the one with the Russian coworker. The man worked later than usual on the morning Larisa disappeared. He looked for her, but she was gone, so he found another employee to give him a ride back to jail, where he promptly checked back in. His story was solid.

Bill's explanation of the flat tires checked out too. Investigators brought the van to a mechanic, who tested each tire and determined that there was no reason any of them should have gone flat. Unless someone tampered with them.

IN EARLY SEPTEMBER 1994, top headlines across the nation focused on the World Series. Due to a strike by Major League players, the series was cancelled for the first time in 90 years. But in the tri-state area around Sioux Falls, people anxiously followed stories about the search for Larisa.

"It might take an outside tip to solve this thing," Lieutenant Folkerts told an *Argus Leader* reporter. To encourage people to come forward, Morrell's and Professional Carpet Systems, where Bill was employed, offered an $8,000 reward.

The community pulled together. Friends and volunteers passed out thousands of flyers asking for citizens to come forward with information about Larisa. The Minnehaha County Emergency Management Office directed a search along railroad tracks, gravel pits, and wooded areas near roads where a vehicle could easily dump a body and get back out quickly. They searched with dogs and helicopters. Dedicated people who believed she was abducted formed an organization called the Friends of Larisa. Many in the group were from the Dumanskys' church, and these friends worked over Labor Day weekend to send out 4,000 letters with Larisa's photo and information. The group took to foot and canvassed the neighborhood. They printed 5,000 cards with her photo and distributed these to stores that sold hunting and fishing licenses, knowing that hunters coming into the state for the upcoming pheasant season would be tramping through outlying fields and thickets.

Sergeant Larry Gulickson led a search team comprised of civil defense volunteers and police along the river, even though they had no direct tip that she was there. It was part of their thoroughness along with using one of the hospital's helicopters to search the area around Sioux Falls. The investigators worked overtime re-interviewing certain coworkers, friends, and family who were of special interest. Detectives put press releases in the newspaper asking for help with clues, including information on Larisa's handmade purse from the Soviet Union which she likely had when she disappeared. Calls came in from psychics wanting to help locate Larisa as well as the typical "crackpot" calls that did nothing but waste investigators' time. They exhausted remote leads and even looked into whether her disappearance had anything to do with the Ringling Brothers Circus, which had been in town the same weekend as her disappearance. Morrell's doubled the amount of reward money, yet the phone calls from citizens offering tips dwindled.

"I can't think of a case where we've worked harder," Folkerts was quoted as saying in the newspaper.

By mid-September the case stalled. Detectives were frustrated and ran out of leads. They couldn't get traction and never felt they were on the cusp of a hot lead. The case would have to be shelved, but Lt. Gary Folkerts planned to continue monitoring similar disappearances throughout the Midwest. None of the investigators involved could forget an unsolved case of this magnitude. It lay just beneath their skin in hopes that some unexpected clue would arise to solve the mystery of her disappearance.

Bill was cleared as a suspect early in the investigation. Though that was an obvious relief, the house seemed airless without Larisa. It was her love of life that added a sparkle to their family. Larisa had embraced this new country with fervor. She learned to speak English quickly and fluently. The family had built a new house a few months earlier. As the sad, lonely days passed, Bill tried to become proficient at household duties that came naturally to Larisa. He eventually learned how to do the laundry and other cleaning but lacked even basic cooking skills. His mother cooked traditional Russian meals for them, and friends regularly brought food to the house. It was the seemingly mundane daily events that tugged at his heartstrings the most, like the day his youngest daughter came running to announce she'd lost her first tooth and wanted to tell her mommy. Every night, he and the children hoped and prayed that Larisa would return.

Days of worry drifted into weeks, then months. Bill left everything in the house just as it was the day his wife disappeared. He couldn't give up hope. Sometimes he'd think he spotted her in a store, but then he'd get closer and realize it wasn't her. Visits from friends tapered off. He assumed it was too uncomfortable for people to come around and not know what to say. The weekends were the hardest; there were just too many hours to fill without Larisa. For the close-knit family, the feeling of waiting on edge became their new normal.

Young Love
Mid-1980s – 1996

WITH ITS SNOW-CAPPED mountains, moss-dripped forests, and winding Owyhee Canyonlands, Oregon beckoned to Vance Streyle with its beauty. He packed up and left the cornfields and prairie grasses of South Dakota for a place where the Pacific waves caress a scalloped shoreline adorned with both rocky and sandy beaches. The scenic cliffs appealed to Vance as a setting where he could continue with higher education. Perhaps nature's peace and beauty would parallel the desires he held for his future. He was excited and optimistic about starting this new chapter in his life. God guided his decision to enter Canyon View Bible School and Seminary, where he planned to become ordained and lead a church someday.

At the same time, Piper Potts, a good-natured and well-liked homecoming queen from Rio Medina, Texas, had committed to attending the same college with similar plans to follow God's Will for her life. Piper was born February 11, 1968. When her father held his newborn baby daughter, he immediately thought she should have a special name. Piper. He liked the first name of actress Piper Laurie and, being an amateur pilot, admired the Piper Cub airplane. Along with her three brothers, the family lived in Ohio for most of Piper's childhood and moved back to Texas before she started high school. Piper threw herself into school activities, playing clarinet, performing with the flag team, and serving as a statistician for the baseball and basketball teams.

As fate would have it, Vance and Piper crossed paths repeatedly. Vance was intrigued with Piper's positive attitude toward life, and he soon found himself hopelessly attracted to this petite, energetic woman with shoulder-length brown hair. Conversations led to their common goals of starting a church, working with children, and organizing a Bible camp where kids could not only have fun but learn about Christ.

Piper was the all-American "girl next door." Vance would later comment, "I met this gal called Piper, and I thought to myself, 'That is some gal. That is the gal I want to marry.'"

Nature took its course; they fell deeply in love and exchanged wedding vows two years later in 1989. Before long, more joy arrived with the birth of daughter Shaina, and two years later a son, Nathan, came along.

The Streyles returned to South Dakota and made their home on a 40-acre piece of rural property west of Sioux Falls. Their home was south of Lake Vermillion, where in summer, tiny wildflowers dotted the grasslands and waves of purple from clover patches added hues of color. In the morning and evening, whitetail deer appeared in the meadows and colorful ring-neck pheasants cackled from the grain fields like a scene from a Terry Redlin painting. Piper and Vance worked diligently to achieve their dreams. They opened Prairie View Bible Camp on their property during the summer. Vance took leave from his plumbing job to work as a camp counselor and Piper, who worked part time, taught Bible lessons to the young campers. They owned a small bus and picked up the day campers each morning and drove them home at the end of each day. The camp offered crafts, archery, and a swimming hole, all interspersed with Bible lessons. Anyone who drove by could see the camp shelter that covered rows of wooden pews which were used on Sundays for outdoor worship. The couple could not have been more pleased with the progress they were making in reaching others with God's Word. Their church was coming to life. Vance and Piper located a Catholic Church down the road that was scheduled for demolition and made plans to purchase it and have it moved to their property. On July 25th, Reverend Terry Weber gave the Streyles the legal papers to take home and sign. Through love and hard work, all of their dreams were falling into place.

A Knock at the Door
Friday, July 26, 1996,
between 8:00 and 9:00 AM

FRIDAY MARKED THE last day of Bible Camp for the season. The Streyle family was preparing for the day when someone knocked at the door.

"I'll get it!" Shaina shouted.

"No, honey, I'll get it," Vance replied, not wanting Shaina to answer the door without knowing who it was. He opened the door and found a young man of average height with a mustache and wearing a black baseball cap. The man seemed visibly startled to see Vance. He fidgeted and shuffled his feet. Vance quickly stepped forward and extended a hand. "I'm Vance Streyle," he said while noting the man's eyes darting back and forth. In the background was a black SUV. Even the tire rims were black.

The man looked out of place and appeared nervous. He hesitated before stammering, "I'm, uh, Robert Anderson." He shook Vance's hand weakly.

"Can I help you?" Vance asked.

The man appeared uncertain about what he wanted to say but finally sputtered, "Uh, do you run a camp or something here?"

Vance proceeded to give the man a pitch about Prairie View Bible Camp and then asked if the man had children.

"Yep. Ages four, three, two, and one," Robert explained. He seemed a bit more at ease. Vance had that effect on people, and the man continued, "My dad lives in Doc Schaefer's place up by Lake Vermillion, so I've driven by here a lot. I figured it must be some kind of camp you run."

The explanation was plausible. The rows of pews were visible from the road. Vance pointed out that they only accepted children five years of age and above. Then he added, "If you give me your name and address, we'll put you on our mailing list." Piper appeared with a pen and notepad. Robert didn't say anything, but his eyes fixed on her. He scratched down some information on the paper and gave it back to Vance. The black SUV drove down the road and disappeared over a hill. The Streyles went to collect their campers, and the day continued with a flurry of archery, swimming, and Bible stories.

A Mean Man Took Nathan's Tent July 29, 1996

SHERIFF TAYLOR MET Vance at the entrance to the driveway.

"What's going on?" Vance asked. The children's babysitter had informed him that Piper called about 9:30 AM and said she was bringing the kids there that afternoon but never showed up. When Vance called for the second time around noon, he left a message saying, "Where are you?" Then he added that if he didn't hear from Piper, he would pick up the kids at the sitter's house.

"We don't know where your wife is, and as of right now, I need you to stay out here and not talk to the kids," Taylor replied. It went unspoken between the two that Vance was currently trapped in the shadows of suspicion. Wearing a white T-shirt and jeans, Vance sat alone by a wooden rail fence next to the driveway. His head hung low, his face cradled in his hands as though distressed. Vance rightfully appeared stunned and dazed at the confusion of not knowing what happened to Piper.

Taylor, Severson, and the other investigators huddled in a tight circle, speaking in low voices. The still air was occasionally broken by the crackle and squelch of a two-way radio from one of the several patrol cars parked in the lane. With the little girl continuing to say that a mean man took her mommy, their gut feeling told them that

Vance had absolutely no part in this. Time is vital in a missing person's case, and with this in mind, the lawmen decided to allow Vance to speak with his children.

Severson went back inside to ask Shaina more questions, but when she saw her daddy at the door, she broke away and ran to him sobbing and clinging to his legs before exploding with information. "Daddy! The mean man took Nathan's tent, but Mommy said it was okay!"

The previous day, Nathan turned two. He received a blue play tent from his parents. It was set up in the bedroom, and the previous night the whole family crawled inside to have their picture taken. In the photo, Vance and Piper are beaming, and Nathan and Shaina sit between them wearing coordinating gingham outfits; Shaina in red, and Nathan in blue. The siblings played in the tent all day, and the gift was clearly a hit.

"There was a loud bang, and Mommy told me to get Nathan and hide! He took Nathan's tent!" she said again.

"It's okay," Vance assured her, trying to make sense of the surreal events. "We'll get Nathan another tent."

"The mean man in the black truck carried Mommy away. She's not coming back." Shaina collapsed in tears.

One of the officers recorded Shaina's comments in a notebook while a roadblock was being set up. Anyone passing by was stopped and questioned regarding anyone or anything they saw at the Streyle residence that day. One of the vehicles they stopped was a county road grader. Driver Donny Theel was in the cab, and he had seen something unusual.

"At about 9:30 AM I was headed south when a flat black SUV with black wheels and CB antenna on the left front came toward me headed north toward Lake Vermillion. It got about 100 yards from my grader when all of a sudden, it pulled a U-turn, went down in the ditch, and sped back to the south." The stark blackness of the vehicle along with its flat coloring caught Theel's observant eye even before the SUV made a sudden turn around. "I drove my grader south a few miles until I hit the county line and then turned around to go north and blade the other side."

"Did you see the SUV again?"

"About an hour later I saw the same SUV come from the west and run a stop sign right in front of me. Then I saw the same vehicle about noon. I was in my cab eating lunch right over there." He pointed to an area across from the Streyles'. "This time the SUV was headed west."

His account confirmed Shaina's mention of a black vehicle. Along with the erratic driving Theel described, the investigative team already had a lead to zero in on. The lab crew arrived, and with Vance helping, they painstakingly moved through the home searching for clues. The home was eerily silent except for the soft *click, click, click* of the crime scene photographer's camera. A box was upended, items were strewn about, and several objects were tipped over. It was difficult to determine if there was a struggle or if the scene was due to two young children and a dog having the run of the house for the day.

When they reached the children's bedroom, they discovered the blue play tent was indeed missing. All that remained were the plastic tent poles as a chilling testament to something being amiss. When Vance was out of earshot, the detectives quickly theorized that the assailant may have taken the tent to dispose of Piper's body. Though logical, the theory would prove to be wildly inaccurate; the true meaning of the missing tent was so critical to the investigation that when it finally came to light, it set into motion a chain of events that would eventually lead to the legal demise of Piper's abductor. One of the investigators floated the obvious idea to check into Piper's coworkers and clients. They would discover that Piper worked primarily with children as a result of her elementary education degree.

Then investigators searched the area outside the Streyle trailer for potential evidence. One of the few items collected was a spent shell casing from a 9mm handgun found in the Streyles' driveway under Sheriff Taylor's vehicle. This shell casing eventually became significant, but on July 29 its value was not apparent. Vance confirmed that he did not own any handguns.

Investigators thoroughly searched the home for two days. Significant finds that the lab personnel bagged included Piper's hairbrush containing several strands of her hair to use for possible evidence. From the bathroom trash, they retrieved bloodstained sanitary pads, though at the time none of them could have realized the importance of this discovery either. Several investigators were out searching abandoned buildings, empty grain bins, and other areas that could hold a body. As the sun faded in the west, so did hopes of locating Piper that evening. A group of agents, including game warden Floyd Demaray, stayed behind to secure the trailer with crime scene tape, to discuss what happened, and to prepare plans about how to find Piper. Severson headed to his office to continue working on the case. There would be no sleep on this long night. Vance scooped his children into his arms, held them even tighter than usual, and then loaded them into the car. They went to Sioux Falls to spend the night with his parents.

A Man Named Robert Anderson
July 29-30, 1996

AT 9:30 PM, Shaina and Nathan were tucked in bed. The initial shock of Piper's disappearance ebbed, and a crucial memory popped into Vance's head. On Friday, a strange man in a black SUV stopped at their home inquiring about Bible Camp. He rushed to the phone and fumbled to call the number he was given by DCI agent Barry Mennenga. Vance relayed to Mennenga that a Robert Anderson had provided his name and address which was on a slip of paper in the trailer house.

"Meet me there as soon as you can. I'm on my way," Mennenga said.

Though it was after midnight, a few people, including Floyd Demaray, were still at the Streyles'. Their commitment to find this young mother was strong. Vance, Mennenga, Severson, and other investigators descended on the residence in an orderly manner, each searching a different area of the home for this slip of paper.

"I know that slip of paper was right in the desk drawer. I don't know why it's not there." Vance was visibly distraught.

After a long search, they were discouraged at being unable to find it. Then Vance explained how he remembered the man's name.

"Robert Anderson is my grandfather's name." Vance also remembered the man saying that his father lived by Doc Schaefer's place close to Lake Vermillion.

As game warden, Demaray not only knew the area but also the residents. Severson knew that Demaray's familiarity with those things could prove useful.

"Is there a Robert Anderson who lives near the lake?" Severson asked.

"There's a Grubby Anderson who lives by Doc Schaefer's house," the warden said. "I believe his real name is Leland, but everyone calls him Grubby."

That was all Mennenga and Severson needed to hear. They rushed back to town, where Severson made a call to the state Department of Motor Vehicles and asked for the records of every black Bronco and similar types of vehicles in the state of South Dakota. Then they ran the records for Robert Anderson and came up with a slew of names so decided to check the name Leland Anderson. Leland had an arrest record which listed Ruth Anderson as next of kin. They obtained Ruth's phone number, and even though it was now 3:00 AM, they fabricated a quick story to get information about Robert Anderson. A DCI agent called her home, and the phone rang repeatedly until a sleepy voice answered.

"Is this Ruth Anderson?" the DCI agent asked.

"Yes. Who is this?"

"Sorry to call at this hour, but I'm an over-the-road trucker and just got into town. Do you have a husband or son named Robert Anderson?"

"I have a son named Robert."

"I'm dealing on buying a car from Robert Anderson. Can I talk to him?"

"Not right now. He's at work. He works the night shift at Morrell's."

The word "Morrell's" made the air go still.

The Bronco
July 30, 1996

THE INVESTIGATORS CALLED Morrell's and obtained Robert Anderson's phone number and address. Even though he should be at work, they drove by his house to see if there was a black Bronco. There wasn't. As a refrigeration technician, Robert worked 11:00 PM to 7:00 AM, which was different than the three typical shifts at the factory. They ran Robert's name through the DMV again using his home address, which revealed a Bronco registered to his name. A group of agents drove through the parking lot at Morrell's to find the vehicle with that license plate. To their dismay, they found the plate, but it wasn't a black vehicle as Donny, the operator of the road grader, described. It was blue with a custom white and black weaved pattern painted on the sides. They were stymied by this unexpected find. It was nearing 5:00 AM, and one of the agents was assigned the task of watching the blue Bronco while the others left to call the road grader operator to ask him to come to the parking lot and identify the vehicle.

After Donny arrived, investigators drove him around the parking lot without revealing any information about the blue Bronco. When they eventually approached this Bronco, Donny asked them to stop.

"If that blue Bronco was black, it would be the vehicle," he said confidently.

His comment confirmed the perplexing find of what seemed to almost be the vehicle for which they were searching. It was as though the last piece of the puzzle didn't fit. Donny left, and one of the agents was assigned to put surveillance on the Bronco. Just after 7:00 AM, a stocky, balding man left in the SUV, unaware he was being tailed by authorities.

Homing In
July 30, 1996

THE BLUE BRONCO careened through the streets in the morning light trailed by DCI agents. The balding man eventually parked and exited the SUV at a white and green trailer house on the west side of Sioux Falls. While one group of agents staked out the Bronco, others were putting together a photo lineup using Anderson's 1994 driver's license picture, which they obtained from DMV records. This was placed with photos of other men who had similar appearances. When the photo lineup was shown to Vance, he disappointingly could not identify with certainty that Anderson was the person who inquired about Bible Camp.

Next, they separated the pictures and, like a deck of cards, showed each to Shaina one at a time. Shaina also could not pick out Anderson as the "mean man who took my mommy."

At that point, there was nothing to tie Anderson to the kidnapping other than the fact that he owned a Bronco, but due to its bright blue coloring, it didn't match the description of the black Bronco for which they were searching. Protocol required the agents to conduct an elimination interview which was, as the name suggests, an interview to eliminate Anderson as a potential suspect. Bob Grandpre, a DCI supervisor, happened to be in Sioux Falls evaluating several DCI agents when he heard about Piper's kidnapping. He offered to conduct the interview to help ease the workload for the agents who were following more important leads, so he went to Anderson's house with the intent of asking him to come to the police station.

Grandpre pounded persistently on the weather-beaten door of the trailer house until it finally opened a few inches. A shirtless man who appeared to have been rousted from sleep appeared in the doorway. Grandpre introduced himself and showed his badge. He felt a surprising twinge of suspicion from merely looking at the man.

"Are you Robert Anderson?"

"Yes."

"I'd like you to come down to the police station for an interview," Grandpre said.

The man nodded, unconcerned. "Okay."

Grandpre paused. Anderson's reaction was completely out of whack. Where were the standard questions? *"What's this about?"* Or *"Am I being charged with something?"* Instead, the suspect quickly dressed and followed Grandpre to the station.

On the drive, the seasoned supervisor changed his strategy based on a growing unease worming its way to the surface. His initial assessments of a suspect's character often proved uncannily accurate, and this innate ability was possibly what led him away from a career in counseling and into law enforcement. During his days as a student at Northern State College in Aberdeen, South Dakota, Grandpre was taking master's classes when he found himself in a bind. He was searching for a way to fit in a full load of classes and long hours of writing papers while still paying the bills.

"You should apply for a night job at the jail," a friend suggested. "You can get paid to babysit inmates all night and write your papers to boot."

Grandpre did and in the process got bitten by the "cop bug." He became a deputy sheriff before advancing to a state special agent. During a chance interview, it became apparent that he had the intuition required to glean information from suspects. Due to this natural ability, he was increasingly called upon to question suspected sex offenders, and his extraordinary success landed him a job as a supervisor. The countless hours spent around sexual predators caused his antennae to go up the moment he saw Anderson's first smirk. If Grandpre's hunches were correct, this suspect would undoubtedly not admit to anything, so several other agents, including lead agent Barry Mennenga, would be involved in the questioning process.

It was a simple room with glossy, white-waxed tile floors and a plain, dark-brown table surrounded by four chairs. The drywall, a light cream color, showed the faintest signs of age with an occasional crack spidering down from the ceiling. Bolted to one wall was a video camera. A one-way mirror allowed observers to watch undetected. DCI agents Grandpre and Mennenga, both veterans with keen skills in observing a suspect's eyes, body language, and voice tones, got the first crack at questioning this person of interest. They paused to look over the balding man seated across the table. He had beady eyes, a smug expression, and a baby-plump build. He was unimpressive despite his attempt to convey shrewd confidence. When asked to state his full name, he replied, "Robert Leroy Anderson."

Suspicious Answers
July 30, 1996

DURING THE FIRST interview with Anderson, not only were Grandpre and Mennenga present but also Fred DeVaney from the DCI, Lt. Gary Folkerts from the Sioux Falls Police Department, and Phil Toft, an investigator from the sheriff's department. Grandpre and Mennenga wasted little time asking preliminary questions. With sober-toned voices and serious stares, they began a series of questions.

"Do you know why we asked you to come down here?" Grandpre asked.

"Well, I suppose it might be about that girl that went missing," Anderson said.

Grandpre and Mennenga immediately knew that was not a standard answer. An innocent person would respond with bewilderment.

"What made you think that's why we wanted to talk to you?" Grandpre shot back.

"I read about it in the paper this morning."

Grandpre was not convinced. It was clear that he'd woken up Anderson back at the trailer.

"Did you stop at the Streyle home on Friday, July 26th? The place is south of Lake Vermillion."

"Uh, yes. I wanted to know about the camp," Anderson replied, unnerved.

"Did you go back to that home on Monday, July 29th?"

"No, I didn't."

The agents wordlessly focused on his expression, then turned their gaze downward to write some notes. Their deliberate hesitations between questions were designed to create anxiety on the part of Anderson. Fluorescent lights hummed above them in the otherwise silent room while they pondered their next question.

"Are you sure you didn't stop at the Streyle place again on Monday?

"I did stop out there like yesterday morning, I guess, around eleven, you know. I didn't see a vehicle. I pulled in, didn't see a vehicle because I remember two vehicles sitting there, so I pulled in…and back out."

In what appeared to be a ploy to buy himself time, Anderson had lit up a cigarette and took a few drags before answering. He was at ease, and possibly enjoyed this game of dangling bits of information in front of the investigators. The man's overconfidence in his story would likely be his downfall. The investigators were not strangers to this and had carefully crafted questions that required Anderson to give quick general answers which were then used to corner him into more specifics.

When asked more details, he switched his story and recalled that he returned to the Streyle home two more times that morning, knocked, but nobody answered. "I wanted to ask if I could use their archery range." He admitted to seeing the road grader and making a U-turn in front of it but had no logical explanation for the U-turn.

"Is there any reason we'd find fingerprints on the door?"

"I did try the doorknob," Anderson said.

With this crucial admission, the arrogant Anderson finally played the wrong card. Grandpre's adrenaline surged. *This guy just put himself at the crime scene. We have the assailant right here, right now.* But none of the agents reacted to the coveted answer and rather acted as though it were insignificant.

"Have you washed or painted your Bronco recently?"

Anderson replied that he had not but had no explanation when asked how his SUV was so clean after driving it on dusty gravel roads. They knocked him off balance. He was struggling to maintain his ruse of being self-assured, so they launched into a set of different questions. Anderson would be rethinking the information he'd just given up about the Streyle home while also having to focus on a separate topic.

"Do you own now or have you ever owned a handgun?"

"No. Never seen the use of a handgun."

The agents exchanged a knowing look. Anderson's answers were suspicious and implausible. A camera was recording the interview while a group of agents sat behind the mirror waiting for Anderson to make a statement that would give them reason to issue a warrant.

So, while Grandpre stretched out the interview, Mennenga left after forty-five minutes to work behind the scenes preparing affidavits for search warrants. It took several hours to prepare the documents and locate a judge. During this time, Anderson regained his footing. The investigators had the distinct impression that their suspect thought he was smarter than all of them, a fact that could work in their favor. Anderson made obvious attempts to control the interview by going off on tangents, talking about his knowledge of black holes in space, the speed of light, the Roman Empire, and theories of physics. Later, he compared his own intelligence to that of Albert Einstein, even claiming he had developed his own theory of light. At times he expressed boredom and started doodling.

"I'm starting to lose my concentration. I'm tired. I knew when you brought me in here if I asked you, you wouldn't let me leave."

"Why did you know that? We let you drive down here," Grandpre countered.

"I just assumed the reason you let me drive down here is because you wanted to go through my Bronco."

"You're way ahead of us."

"No, I'm not," Anderson said, using just three short words to convey that no one could outsmart him, and he knew exactly what the detectives were after.

"The door is open," Grandpre said, indicating that no one was forcing Anderson to stay.

"What door? On the Bronco?"

"No. The door is unlocked." Then the detectives switched course and asked if he knew Larisa Dumansky, to which Anderson replied that he worked with her. He was repeatedly using the same ploy of leading the detectives almost to the answer they wanted before switching course. His skill in doing this led them to wonder if he'd read up on interrogation tactics. One of the detectives left the room briefly and returned saying they needed a photograph of Anderson, so the interview was momentarily stopped. When they returned, DeVaney broke the news to Anderson that they took the telephone answering machine from the Streyle residence. His tone was cutting. "I just listened to a recording of a little girl at home saying, 'Please help me.'" After a pause he then referred to the photos they'd just taken of Anderson. "Any idea why I took those pictures?"

"Well, I suppose you wanted something to show, to verify that it was me that they saw or something like that," Anderson curtly said in a nonchalant manner.

"What's going to happen is I'm going to show that picture to that little girl, and if she tells me that you're the man that took her mommy—"

"I don't see how she could, because I didn't—"

"You don't need to hear it, do you? It's a little girl begging for help."

"You know, whatever your point is, make it." Anderson exhaled long and drawn out, emitting the sound of a bored huff. "I'm getting tired. I have to work. I mean…"

DeVaney hardened and leaned toward Anderson. "I can't believe you're pulling that bull**** on me after I talked to you about this.

You're telling me you're worried about work and sleep, and we're in here making accusations like this? This is like the most important day of your life. Don't be giving me that sh** that you're worried about work, and you're worried about sleep…There's no way that girl did not open that door and come out when you knocked on it, not in the shape she was in. She saw who did this, Rob."

"She did not; she did not come out. The door was not open. I did not go in." Anderson paused deep in thought before finally admitting, "It doesn't look good for me."

Anderson claimed to be tired yet seemed focused and alert. He was not prepared to admit any more, but the investigators needed more. They hoped he would say he opened the door, or he went in, but it was clear that wasn't forthcoming. At some point, a grave realization washed over Grandpre and Mennenga based on the collected bits of information Anderson offered. Piper could still be alive. Without getting Anderson to crack, however, they'd never know. Anderson hadn't been read his Miranda rights because he hadn't been charged. At this point there was enough for a search warrant but not enough to charge him with a crime. If they let him go, he was smart enough to know he'd be followed. If he had Piper locked up somewhere, he might not go back. She could die from dehydration, starvation, or suffocation if he had her in a small enclosure. The priority now was to save Piper if she was still alive. They needed to keep Anderson talking of his own accord. He was free to leave whenever he wanted, but if he left and Piper was still alive, the chances of finding her diminished to almost nothing. Then came the rub. While the beginning of the interview would likely be allowed in court, after the point when Anderson first requested to leave, a judge would rule that anything Anderson said would be inadmissible. So anything Anderson now admitted would likely not be allowed as evidence. If he confessed to the crime, his confession would not be admissible in court. However, the priority was to keep him talking to gain any clues on how to find Piper. Anything else was secondary.

"Do you know anything else about this Piper Streyle?" Grandpre pressed on.

"I read that Piper seemed nice."

Grandpre's adrenaline built every time the interview headed in the wrong direction. He played off whatever Anderson said to get them back on course.

"You said you'd been to the Streyle home before. So, did she seem nice when she handed you a pen?"

Anderson ignored the question about the pen but made a critical admission. "Yeah, I'd drive around after work in the mornings, and I've seen her outside getting the mail."

This game of cat-and-mouse heightened Grandpre's senses, and he fixated with focused concentration on finding the key, the weakness in Anderson's bravado that would unlock the answers they needed. He shuddered at the thought that they might have the chance to save her but that a single misstep could lead to her death. Piper's life could literally be in their hands. Grandpre seamlessly altered his questions and spoke in generic terms the way he did when talking to a sexual predator.

"If someone kidnapped Piper, what do you think they'd do with her?" Grandpre gave Anderson the opportunity to talk about what someone else might have done with Piper in hopes that this would be less threatening.

Anderson perked up. "I've heard that when a woman is abducted, she is tied up and raped. Sometimes she's kept as a sex slave." Anderson responded with a tone of excitement, but he was careful to talk in third person. It was obvious that Anderson was becoming aroused by sharing his ideas of what might happen to a female. There was a look of rapture on his face; he babbled on like an excited child bursting with excitement over an accomplishment.

Anderson spoke frankly about sex for almost two hours, telling what he thought women liked having done to them sexually. He appeared so at ease that it seemed time for the investigators to move to the next level of questioning. Before they could, he again claimed to be tired and suggested he should leave.

"You can leave anytime, but you may want to hear what we just learned."

Anderson went quiet. "What did you learn?"

"We have reason to believe that Piper might be alive."

It was a risky move but one they hoped would give him the green light to tell where they could find, or perhaps recover, Piper. It was worded in a way that gave him permission to admit what happened and end the exhausting questioning. On the other hand, he might get spooked and leave, taking with him all knowledge of Piper's whereabouts or even go and kill her. Anderson didn't bite. The move didn't work, which magnified concern that she was not alive. Then Anderson became bolder, continuing to talk about deviant sex whereas a normal person would have become upset and protested by saying, "Look, I didn't do it!" When Anderson again asked to leave, the agents stalled by taking a break out of earshot of Anderson.

"I'm done unless we Mirandize him," Grandpre said. Reading the Miranda rights would mean that Anderson could not leave, but he still would not be under arrest.

"If we do that, he could get spooked and refuse to talk further. He could ask for a lawyer, and this could drag out. In the meantime, Piper could die," an agent countered.

The decision was made to try to bait him into staying longer. Grandpre took a moment to pray the words he spoke each time before interrogating a suspect. *God, I can't do this unless I get your help and guidance.* He couldn't go it alone and asked God to stay with him. Sometimes interviews ran ten to twelve hours. Grandpre's strategy was to keep talking as long as the suspect would keep going. During that time, he had to hear sickening and infuriating confessions but had to act as if he understood so the offender wouldn't shut down. It was Grandpre's unwavering belief that he could not do this with his own strength but only through endurance from a higher power.

When the agents reentered the room, Anderson sat with a half-smirk as if anticipating their next move.

"You can go, Robert, but we have a question. We're hearing that you may have knowledge about Piper's whereabouts. Can you help us out with that?"

He couldn't but instead talked about black holes and his knowledge of engineering. It was a high-stakes chess game, and every skilled move made by the detectives was cunningly countered by Anderson. The detectives requested that he take a polygraph test, but he refused on the grounds that he didn't consider it reliable. The game was over. They had held him for eight hours and gathered little useful knowledge. Eventually, they gave Anderson the news that he could not go back to his home or get into his vehicle, as they had obtained warrants to look for evidence.

"We don't want those areas disturbed until we have the opportunity to search them."

Anderson protested and reiterated his innocence, telling them he was in the wrong place at the wrong time looking for a Bible Camp. His demeanor softened, and in a falsely helpful tone, he told one of the investigators, "You'll need to jiggle the handle on the Bronco to get it open because it sticks." It was a desperate attempt to gain some control over the situation. Then, with the warrants in place, a gaunt-looking Anderson was directed to relinquish the clothes he was wearing, including a fanny pack, per the requirements of the search warrant. Inside his fanny pack, agents found a key ring with two handcuff keys attached. They took his blood, hair, and fingernail samples. During the strip search, they took extensive notes, including the fact that Anderson did not have on underwear. It was a detail that would later link him to Piper's disappearance.

Suspicious Items
July 30–August 1, 1996

SIOUX FALLS LAW enforcement went to work scouring Anderson's Bronco while other investigators broke into teams and searched his home, storage shed, and Anderson himself. The Bronco immediately emitted a slew of suspicious finds. It was littered with bags, trash, boxes, and the assorted tools and gear one might expect to find in the possession of an adult male. Due to being both a slob and packrat, Anderson unintentionally provided agents with a trail of his recent activities through the collection of months of bags and receipts. There were two invoices of particular interest: one showing the purchase of a CB antenna and another for the installation of the antenna the following day.

A receipt from Ace Hardware indicated that on July 25, 1996, someone purchased a pair of brown jersey gloves, two household sprayers, and a three-inch paintbrush. This was followed by the discovery of a pair of brown gloves, now soiled and containing some unknown hairs, possibly from an animal. There was another receipt from the same day but at a different store that showed the purchase of a hand sprayer, a skein of red yarn, and a compact disc. Later that day, agents uncovered a purchase receipt from yet another store for a 16-ounce bottle of 393 craft paint.

The fact that at least three trips had been made to three different stores the day before Anderson's Friday visit to the Streyle home indicated a strong possibility that the items were connected to the crime. A receipt dated July 26 at 12:01 PM attached to a fast food bag containing a half-eaten sandwich added to the suspicion because there was black paint on the sack. A receipt from Menards on July 29 at 8:13 AM, less than three hours before he admitted stopping at Piper's house, showed the purchase of duct tape, a three-inch brush, and a five-quart bucket. So, what did craft paint, paintbrushes, sprayers, and duct tape have to do with Piper's disappearance? Of special interest was the duct tape. Was this receipt for the almost complete roll of duct tape that was found in the Bronco? An agent brought the receipt to Menards and showed it to the clerk along with the photo lineup.

"Do you recognize any of these as the person who made this purchase?"

The clerk scrutinized the pictures before shaking her head no.

A few weeks later, the store manager would call with surprising information that Anderson's check bounced for the July 29 purchase.

WITHIN THE CLUTTER of the Bronco were many other items which would become compelling evidence. The agents were working almost around the clock running down as many leads as quickly as they could because they still did not have sufficient evidence to arrest Anderson. More clues would be revealed when the Bronco was eventually sent to the state crime lab staff for a painstaking and time-consuming search, but for now the Sioux Falls team continued investigating. They discovered crucial evidence in the two toolboxes still untouched in the back end of the vehicle. Based on the strange contents found in one of the toolboxes, agents felt the items were for sinister purposes. They began referring to the box as "the torture kit."

"What the hell did he use these for?" an agent asked, holding up a handful of long, wooden dowels.

Incubation of a Sexual Sadist

Sexual arousal by inflicting pain, suffering, and humiliation on another human being. The need to control, dominate, invoke fear, and subject a sexual partner to aggressive, hostile treatment. Experiencing persistent fantasies that involve inflicting pain on another person. Treatment of the disorder is generally ineffective. These are common descriptions of a sexual sadist—a side of Anderson known to few.

Robert Leroy Anderson was born in Sioux Falls, South Dakota, in 1969 and was the product of a dysfunctional family. He had two brothers and a younger sister. Anderson attended Axtell Park Junior High and went on to Washington High School, where he qualified for a gifted and talented program. Like his brothers, he inherited from his father, Leland, not only a self-centered nature but also the tendency for unlawful behavior. The relationship between Robert and his father would forever be complicated and filled with tension. As though tellingly, Robert listed "Cat's in the Cradle" by Harry Chapin as one of his favorite songs.

The Anderson family was fraught with dysfunction. One of his brothers, Billy, served prison time for manslaughter. Anderson's older brother, Lee Iver, worked as a handyman for Elwood Anderson (no relation), the owner of several rental properties. One night, Lee Iver found himself penniless. He tried to borrow money for cigarettes from a 14-year-old girl who turned him down. Desperate, he broke into the home Elwood shared with his fiancée, Carol Daniels, and attacked the couple in their sleep. He went after Elwood first, stabbing him seven times in the throat, chest, and hands with a seven-inch buck knife. Carol was stabbed on both hands. At some point in the struggle, the knife became lodged in Elwood, causing Lee Iver to panic and run off. Elwood nearly died, and it took forty-two units of blood to save his life. In February of 1997, Lee Iver was found guilty and given a life sentence. He was deemed a habitual offender due to previous felonies. While in the army, he was convicted of rape and before that served time for grand theft. The day would come when Leland and his three sons would all be incarcerated in the South Dakota Penitentiary at the same time.

During high school, the family problems spiraled, and when Robert Anderson's friend Glen Walker and his family decided to move to Kansas City, Anderson moved with them at the beginning of his junior year. Despite this start in a new environment, Anderson eventually dropped out of school. Anderson was intelligent, however, and earned a general education diploma. He bounced around to various jobs, including one at Worlds of Fun Amusement Park in Kansas City. In his early twenties he enrolled in a college engineering program. Professors were impressed by his abilities and commented favorably on his academic performances. He began sharing with a few close friends his peculiar craving for aggressive, harm-inflicting sex. Walker saw red flags regarding Anderson's deviancies. It was during junior high that Anderson first brought up the idea of kidnapping a woman, but Walker wrote it off as "guy talk." Another friend admitted that Anderson's favorite topic of conversation was about kidnapping women. But by the time he reached adulthood, his dark fantasies were nurtured by indulging in bondage and sadomasochistic pornography. He spent increasing amounts of time envisioning ways to bind a female and administer a variety of sexual indignities. He fantasized about a neighbor, coworker, or someone who crossed his path on a regular basis. As time passed, he obsessed over a particular female. In his relentless fantasies he imagined ways to abduct this object of his desire and carry out his deviant sexual cravings. The thrill of the stalk and imagining the abduction was enough to gratify his compulsive thoughts. After many years, simply imagining these sexual lusts was no longer enough to satisfy his dark appetite, and Anderson began putting into motion the plans for his visions to become reality. Years of plotting led him to one conclusion; he needed a partner in crime to carry out the plan, and so he set his sights on a longtime friend.

Stained Jeans, Torture Kit, and Bondage Board
July 30, 1996

SITUATED IN A rough-hewn area, Anderson's trailer house was battered, with faded green and white weather-worn paint flaked here and there. An assortment of trash lay scattered around it. The trailer was located on the west side of town just off the interstate, which made it a quick drive to the Lake Vermillion area. Some of the officers arranged for Anderson's wife and children to join him at a hotel until the search was complete. They did not yet have cause to arrest him. The house was in disarray, with boxes, piles of clothing, and baskets scattered askew. On a wall speaker sat an oversized roll of duct tape. The hallway was nearly impassable due to the heaps of jumble and junk. In one pile of dirty clothes was a pair of blue jeans with grass stains on the knees. Inside the jeans near the crotch was a dark, discolored stain. Investigators even took the vacuum cleaner bag. From the washing machine they collected a pair of wet jeans along with bits of leaves.

Elsewhere, police detectives completed their dissection of the Bronco. In the far back, the team recovered an army entrenching tool with dirt on it along with a walkie-talkie, a large flashlight, and a soiled pair of brown jersey gloves. One of the two toolboxes contained typical tools. The second did not. Inside the first layer was a can of black spray paint, a can of red spray paint, a five-inch tear gas container, nylon straps, and about nine feet of chain. The second layer of the box revealed an X-Acto knife, eyebolts, small pieces of some unknown plants, and several quarter-inch wooden dowels cut into nine-inch pieces. The contents appeared to be items used for torture. The bizarre purpose of these wooden dowels would not come to light until nearly a year later. Investigators felt that if luck was on their side, the leafy weeds had the potential to narrow the scope of the crime scene. On the other hand, if the results showed them to be common plants, it would be hard to narrow the search. The fresh vegetation was promptly sent off to the botany department at South Dakota State University.

By now, the back end of the SUV was largely cleared out and inventoried, which led the agents to a disturbing find. The backseats had been removed, and the reason why became horrifyingly clear. A large, carpeted platform with eye rings in the corners was fitted precisely to the back of the SUV. It looked like a bondage board. One thing that puzzled the investigators was that they could see something had been placed on the bondage board and spray painted which left rectangular-shaped shadows. The Sioux Falls Police Department lab team employed a precise technique to extract small particles from the carpet on the bondage board. After covering the windows of the Bronco, a special light was turned on which made foreign objects glow. They searched every inch of the carpeted board and used tweezers to remove what appeared to be four human hairs, and it was probable that these hairs could be valuable to the case. The five rectangular pink and gray stains on the carpeted board raised little suspicion. Each item, however, would become important, and the spray-painted silhouettes crucial.

The next day the Bronco was towed to the state crime lab in Pierre for another search. The forensic team found something that was missed in Sioux Falls. Considering the amount of clutter and debris piled in the vehicle, it was understandable. Stuck to the bondage board was a scrap of black-and-white cotton cloth. The find would be another key in proving Anderson's guilt.

Then investigators conducted a search of Anderson's backyard shed. This yielded a Menards plastic sack containing a new, unused pair of brown jersey gloves with the label still attached, one can of black spray paint, one can of primer spray paint with a Campbell's Supply price tag, and a nearly complete roll of duct tape. There was also one curious item. It was a 1½ x 5-inch piece of stainless steel. On one end, someone welded a 1½-inch triangle of sharp metal that was spray painted gray. Was this object a homemade weapon? Was it used to inflict pain? The metal concoction was baffling, and its purpose would not soon be solved. The unusual item was tagged and seized, but there was so much clutter that agents had to use their best knowledge to decide what to take as evidence and what to photograph but leave behind. Investigators would eventually return to the shed as items left behind revealed their significance.

Preparations

IN A DOCUMENTARY about predators, a hungry lion stalks and lies in wait. It sets its sights on a single, vulnerable gazelle, and when the opportunity arises, the lion strikes and crushes the life from its helpless prey. The rapist and killer operate in much the same way but are driven by lust rather than survival. The killer plans and prepares. And Robert Anderson did this obsessively.

Rolling conveyor belts transporting pork portions for packaging crisscrossed the massive processing room amid loud clatters. Beneath the clamor, Anderson repaired a broken refrigeration unit. His mind was only partially on the job while his eyes peered at the female workers busy on the assembly line. When finished repairing the unit, he strolled down vacant corridors and stepped through a heavy metal door. He locked himself into the factory's now empty workshop.

Against company policy, Anderson repeatedly used this room for personal projects. As a refrigeration technician, he had keys and access to the shop. When it was empty, Anderson would slip off and let himself in. With the grinder whining, he perfected his devious creation beneath a shower of sparks. He ground a triangular piece of metal against the abrasive wheel until it was needle sharp. Then he used a welder to bond the sharp point to a flat base so that the triangle was in a vertical position.

He again used the shop to make the bondage board to precisely fit the back of his Bronco. He cut a sheet of ½-inch plywood and drilled holes in the corners where he bolted in eye rings. He pulled and pushed on the eye rings to test their sturdiness. They held solid. The rings would surely do their job against the tugs of a struggling female attached by handcuffs. He completed the board by gluing a piece of indoor-outdoor carpeting to the surface. His job provided him the freedom to move around the factory and coworkers noted that Anderson sought out reasons to go to rooms where animals were slaughtered while only somewhat trying to hide the thrill he got from watching the blood spill.

Anderson worked the night shift, and after clocking out, he would often stop by his friend Jamie Hammer's house. The two had known each other since early childhood, so Anderson felt comfortable sharing his sexual plans.

"It would be so easy to follow a woman walking down the sidewalk, come up behind her, throw her into the backseat, tie her down, then haul her to a secluded area and rape her," Anderson said.

Hammer listened, sometimes nodding but rarely making a comment. He was more interested in talking about cars than deviant sex.

"Another idea I'm working on is to flatten the tire of a girl so I can kidnap her. Once she's isolated, she's an easy grab." Anderson's eyes had a wild look, and the corners of his mouth formed a devious smirk. He was gradually drawing Hammer into his plan for the sole reason that he thought it vital to have an accomplice. "You can help me grab her and join in the fun. We'll cut her clothes off and rape her."

Hammer didn't disagree, yet wasn't convinced his friend was serious even when Anderson produced a set of walkie-talkies which he said they would use to abduct a girl. Anderson explained how they would hide along a highway down the road from each other. When the first man observed a lone woman drive by, he'd radio to the other man to place the popper in the path of the approaching vehicle. After the victim hit the tire popper, she'd have to pull over, and the first man would drive up pretending he was there to help but would instead force her into his car.

After repeatedly bringing up the idea of trying this out, Anderson talked his longtime friend into going out in two vehicles to practice with the walkie-talkies and tire poppers. Hammer decided to go along thinking that would finally satisfy his lifelong friend's relentless requests. But to Anderson, the thrill of practicing only escalated his urges.

Hammer's neighbor, June Pederson, often stopped over in the mornings. Both she and Hammer had been unemployed for several months. Anderson frequently discussed sexually related topics in her presence, and the theme grew darker. His conversations focused almost exclusively on violent, deviant, and sadistic sexual acts. In the summer of 1995, he pulled out a 9mm pistol, which he displayed as though it were show-and-tell. June grew weary of the whole scene, and when she left, she kept the strange conversations to herself.

THE TWO FRIENDS spent considerable time together. Three or four times a week they drove around the countryside and through Colton, Chester, Egan, Sherman, and back to Sioux Falls. Anderson drove and would inevitably launch into conversations related to kidnapping a woman. Unknown to Hammer, Anderson had his eye on several women he wanted to rape from these rural towns. Hammer didn't take Anderson's bizarre conversations seriously. He considered them nothing more than the dirty trash talk he heard for years when working on construction crews. Then one day, Anderson attempted to get Hammer to help him kidnap and rape a woman.

"I have some women picked out to abduct," Anderson shared with Hammer. "I've been following one, so I'll drive by and show you where she lives." Anderson drove to the nearby town of Sherman, South Dakota, located just a few miles northeast of Sioux Falls. Cruising past a small house, Anderson pointed.

"She lives right there, but she has a big boyfriend. Another way to get her is to take her right out of the house at gunpoint some night." Anderson continued with details of the plan while he drove Hammer around the countryside, pointing out secluded locations to take his captives and sexually assault them. He discussed ways to dispose of the bodies that included burying them in remote places or dismembering the corpses. Anderson wanted his friend's help to snatch the female, but Hammer flat out told him no.

Undeterred, Anderson bided his time and on a different day brought Hammer with him when he followed a woman back to her home in Egan. Once again, he tried to secure Hammer's help in abducting the woman so they could take turns restraining and raping her. Again, Hammer refused.

Washable Paint
August 1, 1996

A WHIRLWIND OF investigative work took place simultaneously. During the interview with Anderson, agents noticed that he looked much different in person than on his driver's license, which was the image used in the first photo lineup. Since that time, his hairline receded, and in the driver's license picture he was not wearing a hat. Could this be why Vance and Shaina could not pick him out of the photo lineup? Agents took new photos of Anderson with his hat on and put it in a lineup with photos of people also wearing baseball caps to construct a new photo lineup. When the new pictures were shown to Vance, he immediately identified Anderson as the man who stopped by inquiring about Bible Camp. Using the same deck-of-cards approach with Shaina as they had before, she also identified Anderson as the mean man who took her mommy.

The forensic team from the Sioux Falls Police Department moved from examining the inside of the Bronco to the outside and quickly noticed something uncommon. There were drips of black paint along the white tire rims, and when they opened the hood of the vehicle, more drips and splotches of black paint, along with brush marks, could be found on pieces of metal. The paint flecked off with a fingernail rub, so the substance was not standard auto body paint.

A review of the numerous items they removed from the Bronco led them to sales receipts from Ben Franklin dated July 25, 1996, for the purchase of 393 craft paint and Menards, for duct tape, a five-quart paint bucket, and a three-inch paintbrush. DCI agent Earl Miranda went to Ben Franklin and asked for 393 craft paint. Clerk Julie Bradfield handed him a sixteen-ounce bottle of black, water-based paint. He showed Julie the receipt to make sure the bottle of paint he had was the same as the one on the receipt, to which Julie replied that it was.

"Would this paint wash off a vehicle?" he asked.

Julie looked at Miranda with surprise. "You know, you're the second person to ask me that question this week."

"Who was the other person?"

"A man came in and said he was going to paint a friend's car as a prank. We talked about diluting the paint with water and that he'd need a spray bottle to apply it. We don't carry those, so I told him to check Kmart."

"Do you think you could identify a photograph of the person who bought this?"

"I'll try," she responded.

When shown the pictures in the lineup, she identified Anderson as the customer. The mystery of the black SUV revealed its first clue, and Anderson had almost literally painted himself into a corner.

The Find
July 29, 1996,
approximately 1:30 PM,
the day of Piper's abduction

JOEL WUDEL, AN employee at Augustana College in Sioux Falls, was silently reflecting on the fragility of life while driving home from a funeral on Highway 115, a few miles from Baltic, South Dakota. Up ahead on the road he detected a black-and-white object, possibly a referee's shirt, so he slowed the car for a better look. It was a piece of fabric and was located so close to his vehicle that all he had to do was open the door and pick it up without even getting out. Curiously, it was a black-and-white T-shirt that had been cut in half. He stuffed it under the front seat, thinking that since he went to the trouble to pick it up, he might as well use it as a rag to clean his car. He drove off, never imagining there was any significance to the piece of cloth. During his hectic work schedule, he didn't think about it again.

A Community Rallies
August 1, 1996

AN EXTENSIVE SEARCH of the area from which Piper disappeared was organized. Locals, law enforcement, and people from hundreds of miles away poured into the epicenter of the search, an open field fringed with swaying prairie grasses. Many came on their day off; some even requested a leave from work to help look for Piper. A line of school buses from a temporary command center at Lake Vermillion brought more volunteers, who mingled in the morning sun awaiting their assignments from DCI agent Jim Severson. Sheriff Taylor and his deputy Mark Norris coordinated information and tasks coming from the command center and would log evidence throughout the search. Shortly after 9:00 AM, Severson addressed the citizenry.

"You're looking for a possible body, and you're also looking for possible evidence. It might be evidence, and it might not. We're looking for *anything* out of the ordinary."

He explained the logistics of the quest. They would be combing through a thirty-six-square-mile area surrounding the Streyle home. It was divided into nine sections, and those in attendance were assigned an area to search headed by a small crew of law enforcement officials.

"This is probably our only shot at this, to get this concentrated of a search," Sheriff Taylor emphasized. For Taylor, his wife, Lois, and three daughters, the search was a family effort. A typical day found Lois dispatching calls from their home that came into the sheriff's office. But on this day, she was busy assisting with the search for Piper. Their daughter Lisa, who was eight months pregnant, was given a quick lesson on fielding calls coming into the office, and she would handle the duties of the dispatcher. Taylor knew there was a lot of competition among the media to get the latest story, especially during this high-profile search. "When a call comes in, tell them you don't have any information regarding the Streyle case," Taylor instructed Lisa. If a routine call came in, she was to contact him via radio. Taylor's other two daughters, Kim and Sheri, along with their husbands, joined the swelling crowd of searchers.

Some volunteers set out on horseback, trudging up and down steep ravines to examine ground nearly impassable on foot. Above, a helicopter hovered and flew in circular patterns. Searchers waded in murky bog waters, plodding along thick reeds and cattails hampered by their feet sinking into muddy muck. As the sun rose in the sky, so did the humidity, while clouds of mosquitoes descended. The insect repellant they were instructed to use washed away in beads of sweat and did little to discourage the swarming insects that flew in their eyes and bit at any piece of exposed skin. Near a wooded grove, someone discovered a plot of soil that had recently been disturbed, and shouts for a shovel rang across the field. A lead officer examined the area, but it was soon determined to be the work of a badger.

Every abandoned building, common in farming areas, was searched and then picked through again to ensure that nothing was missed. Moving through heavily wooded areas and tall cornfields, searchers shouted to each other, using their voices to stay oriented. On the flatlands needle-sharp thistles scraped their skin, and slimy, moss-covered rocks along waterways made footing treacherous. Eight hours later the assortment of finds was deposited into several boxes as potential evidence but no newsworthy breakthroughs.

For the next week, the DCI followed up leads that continued to mount. Two psychics even offered their visions of where Piper was. The leads were taken seriously but turned up nothing. Sheriff Taylor put the word out that they would continue looking for Piper on Saturday, August 10th, and asked for more volunteers. They also called for people to bring dogs that could work in a big crowd and be able to search for a scent.

Anderson's lawyer scoffed at the search, saying, "Based on evidence, they don't have that strong of a case at this point. And that's why they're out there looking for more evidence. I talked to (Anderson), and he looked me straight in the eye and categorically denied he did this crime."

THEY CAME 500 strong, including the Governor of South Dakota, Bill Janklow. The volunteers arrived ready to go on foot, on horseback, by boat, in ultralight airplanes, and in a helicopter. Nearly forty dogs came to assist. Many counties had search and rescue units with dogs trained to go into culverts, crevices, and thick brush impenetrable to people. A human body gives off a scent until it is completely decomposed, so some of the dogs were brought to lakes and rivers, where they would be able to detect a body even if it was deep below water. This was a small army of communal love with one goal in mind: find Piper and bring her home. One searcher, Gary Schallenkamp, commented on the main reason for so many people showing up.

"That's why a lot of us live in rural South Dakota. It's not supposed to happen here."

The search was narrowed from nine areas to five. People walked nearly shoulder-to-shoulder across flatlands, through ravines and tight rows of corn with green leaves that were deceivingly sharp and left slices like paper cuts. Pollen swelled their eyes. Hour after weary hour they pushed on. Occasionally the helicopter would land if soil was spotted that appeared to have been disturbed.

Local businesses donated so much food that it took sixty women from a nearby church just to assemble a meal for the volunteers. As the sheriff's wife, Lois took it upon herself to deliver the lunch sacks to those in the fields. The crime continually tugged at her heart as she watched her husband and Deputy Norris operate on four hours of sleep a night while working the case. "As a mother, I can't imagine how someone could take Piper away from her two little children and just leave them there all alone," she said.

Throughout the search, suspicious items to be checked for fingerprints were placed into boxes. When their day ended at 5:30 PM, disappointment ebbed. A sense of dismay fell across the people, who had started the day with high hopes of finding something of importance. It would be the last search until the crops were harvested, and they could better navigate the fields. Investigators were buried in a mountain of leads that needed to be followed. The crowd of volunteers thinned; dog owners herded their exhausted hounds into kennels and disappeared down winding roads. Governor Janklow thanked everyone for their efforts. Soon only a handful of law enforcement officers were left, and they too went home except for Sheriff Taylor who couldn't bring himself to stop searching, thinking *we're going to find her.* Being the first law enforcement officer on the crime scene and with the case falling in his jurisdiction, it all felt personal. Walking toward the setting sun, he backtracked alone through fields and draws until the night became so black, he had no choice but to turn around.

But the search for Piper did not end. Friends plastered flyers around the tri-state area on business windows and community bulletin boards that read "ABDUCTED: Piper Jean Streyle," with a picture of a beautiful, smiling woman. The community wondered, *Who is Piper?* While she remained missing, her high school classmates in Texas gathered for a ten-year reunion with a celebration that turned somber. Piper had returned the questionnaire sent out by the reunion committee with cheerful responses. *Are you in the place in life you expected to be 10 years ago?* one of the questions read. After high school, Piper imagined she would have a big career and replied that she was thankful her life took her to where she was instead.

Then in mid-November a mysterious, handwritten note was mailed to authorities with a tip to look below two bridges near Lake Vermillion west of Parker. It included a sketching of water and a bridge. The note read in part:

"You have two bridges west of Parker, South Dakota, like this one. You are looking for her body. Should be there. Good luck. God be with you."

But there happened to be three bridges in the vicinity. Wading through chest-deep water, a search and rescue team probed the bottom and along the banks near all three bridges. The painstakingly slow process turned up nothing, and searchers had to remove the blood-sucking leeches attached to their skin.

Scuba divers searched Lake Vermillion after two men told authorities that they reeled in what appeared to be strands of human hair when fishing. As with other searches, the divers surfaced empty-handed. A seemingly endless stream of leads was followed but did not bring Piper home. Frustration mounted with each promising lead that ended with a fizzle.

Tightening the Investigative Noose

ANDERSON REPEATEDLY CLAIMED to have never owned a handgun. Through numerous interviews of employees at Morrell's, investigators turned up evidence contrary to this claim. At Morrell's, DCI agents spoke with Richard Frye, an employee and acquaintance of Robert Anderson.

"One day Rob came along with me when I went pheasant hunting by Lake Vermillion. I went off to hunt, and Rob stayed at the shooting range near the parking area. He had a 9mm pistol, and he target practiced while I was gone. When we went to leave, he said something weird. Rob pointed out a valley with overgrown bushes and trees. He said it would be a great place to bury a body so it would never be found. I said, 'What are you saying that for?' Rob said, 'I'm only joking, but it would.'" Frye expressed his disgust to Anderson and refused to ever hunt with him again.

Investigators received a tip that led them to another Morrell's employee, Ken Loeffler, who told them that in the fall of 1995, he and Anderson went to the same public shooting range a few miles northeast of the Streyles. Anderson produced a 9mm pistol and did some target practice while Loeffler hunted. Loeffler was able to guide law enforcement to this public shooting area. Using metal detectors, they searched for 9mm shell casings and found twelve of them mixed among a scattering of .22, .45, .357, and other shells that had sunk below the ground over the years. Mike Daugherty, a ballistics expert with the state crime lab, compared the twelve to the spent 9mm cartridge found in the driveway of the Streyle home the day Piper disappeared. Eleven of the twelve firing pin marks from the cartridges found at the shooting range matched the casing from the driveway. It was a victory that would add to the accumulating circumstantial evidence, but it was far from enough to clinch the case. They were still missing the proverbial "smoking gun."

Duct Tape
Late September 1996

THE RESULTS CAME in regarding the vegetation from the torture toolbox found in the Bronco. Dr. Gary Larson from the SDSU Botany Department identified it as black snakeroot and honewort.

"These plants only grow along a riverbank where there is a lot of shade and no grazing," he explained.

"If we took you around, could you point out where these plants might be found?" the agent inquired.

Knowing the importance of the case, Gary agreed to help. The search for Piper was focused around the town of Montrose and Lake Vermillion, as these were areas where the black SUV was seen on the day Piper went missing. By now, agents determined Anderson had painted his Bronco black with the washable tempera paint. To expedite the search for the black snakeroot and honewort, the agents secured a helicopter and pilot. With Gary on board, the aircraft was airborne and headed west. They circled the Lake Vermillion area, and the botanist pressed his face against the window and studied the terrain below with only the steady *whump whump whump* of the main rotor to break the silence. Nobody on the aircraft spoke. Finally, he shook his head.

"These plants would not be found in this area. I suggest we search along the Big Sioux River."

The pilot swung to the east and maneuvered the aircraft along the Big Sioux. They lumbered along doing a visual search for shady areas not adjacent to grazing land. It was near September, and a green stripe of mature, leafy trees along both sides of the river blocked the view of the plants and shrubs along the water. Near the town of Baltic, Gary identified an area he deemed worthy of searching. The helicopter hovered, then swung over to Baltic and slowly descended; the down blast created a whirlwind of dust, debris, and sticks thrown in all directions. Once landed, the group proceeded along the river. Gary pointed out sections that showed all the conditions conducive for the growth of black snakeroot and honewort.

"I'd be looking right here," he said.

His words were golden, and it seemed even nature was assisting the agents with this case. The DCI agent made a call to the rest of his team.

"We've been looking in the wrong area."

IT WAS IMPERATIVE to find any evidence, as the approaching autumn weather would soon drop a blanket of leaves making future finds nearly impossible. A group of police volunteers picked their way through the briars and underbrush beneath the towering mass of shade trees along the Big Sioux River. The ill-lit ground made small items difficult to see, and footing became tricky along the slope of the riverbank. The parcel to be searched was too massive an area for a few DCI agents, so all available law personnel were recruited to help with the search. They walked in line, methodically slapping away mosquitoes and picking off wood ticks before they could bore into the skin. After trampling through thickets and clawing their way through fallen branches and decomposing vegetation, a shout went up from a detective who found a torn piece of duct tape. It was the same color of tape as what had been confiscated from Anderson's property. The investigators gathered around the discovery and discussed the next step. The place had a macabre feel, and there was no reason for duct tape to be in this area. They needed a more intensive search with additional help.

The National Guard was contacted. Major Ted Johnson, a military support officer, activated his response team that was trained to assist in crisis situations. Wearing camouflage fatigues and orange safety vests, they walked nearly arm to arm, stooping to rake through branches, weeds, and swampy lowlands. At times they stalled, breaking through eight-foot-tall cattails. They used the technique of having one person place a hat atop a tall stick held high in the air to assist the team in keeping their bearings while staying in a line.

An encouraging shout rang out at the discovery of another wadded-up piece of duct tape. This piece had several hundred strands of human hair attached, and next to it was half of a black-and-white-striped T-shirt which was cut and ripped from the neck to the bottom. It matched the description of the nightshirt Piper was wearing on the morning she was abducted. The shirt was crucial yet disheartening. It solidified the spot as ground zero for the crime. They ended the day with the discovery of a battery-operated vibrator and about 100 yards out, a half-burnt orange candle. In order to properly preserve the evidence, whenever a National Guardsman found an item, he called out. A detective wearing gloves would proceed to the area and seal the item in an evidence bag labeled with the location of the discovery. The finds had the effect of both bolstering the investigation and casting a grim shadow over it.

Despite the detectives' vast experience handling crimes up close, they reeled at the heinous nature of the items that lay before them.

The wad of duct tape and the partial T-shirt were transported to the state crime lab for examination. The duct tape was carefully unrolled, and the jagged end was compared to the torn end of the duct tape roll recovered from Anderson's Bronco. Like a puzzle, the two jagged ends matched perfectly. Samples of the hair stuck to the duct tape were compared to hairs from Piper's hairbrush. They matched. The evidence was stacking up against Anderson. Their focus turned to the odd piece of stainless steel with the triangular point. Speculation rippled through the department as to what its purpose was and how it was connected to the crimes.

***

BASED ON THE crucial evidence found by the police volunteers and National Guard, it was decided to comb the area again, this time with two German shepherds, Marianne and Coyote. The dogs came in from Redmond, Washington, with their trainer, Andy Rebmann, a retired police officer. As the owner of K-9 Specialty Search Associates, his services were in such high demand that he was forced to turn away most requests. Yet, when he did agree to search, he only asked to have his expenses reimbursed and charged nothing more. Marianne and Coyote were trained to locate the scent of decaying bodies and previously had found remains buried five feet deep. Marianne would sniff vigorously for thirty minutes while Coyote rested, and then they'd trade roles. For two days, the dogs scoured the area along the river near Baltic and made occasional finds, including a dead, burned beaver, a tennis shoe, and a buffalo skull. Although the finds were not significant, it was successful in that the need to search the same area again was eliminated.

At one point, authorities brought in NecroSearch International to look for Piper. The highly trained volunteers specialized in finding secretly buried bodies and accumulated an impressive record of assisting in more than sixty murder cases. One member of the team was an entomologist; this scientist who studies insects would be looking for coffin flies, brown beetles, and many other species that are attracted to a dead body. The team brought with them two dogs trained to sniff out decomposing flesh even if it was buried deep in the earth or underwater. The group was not paid but needed accommodations, so a local man offered to move out of his expansive home temporarily, so the non-profit group would have a place to use for headquarters and lodging. The willingness of complete strangers locally and from hundreds of miles away to help was testament that the moral fabric of society was still intact.

The group started out strong under a hot summer sky but quickly found the terrain challenging. Towering brush and prairie grasses hindered their progress. Then a piercing shout from one of the members brought them to a quick stop. One of the searchers stumbled upon a beekeeper's hives and suddenly angry bees began stinging anyone within reach. After a first-aid break, they continued only to encounter ticks, bugs, and the ever-present swarms of mosquitoes. The area to be searched was immense, and the pace was at best plodding. Like the searchers before them, NecroSearch International did not find the missing woman.

Assistance from the Media

AUTHORITIES COULD ONLY release snippets of information surrounding Piper's disappearance, hence not to jeopardize the investigative process, and so the limited news stories did not quench the public's worried curiosity. In a crowded eatery, Celine Dion's popular hit "Because You Loved Me" played from a radio in the back, but the chatter of conversation overshadowed the music. Over cups of hot coffee, citizens discussed what might have happened to the young mother of two. People in this peaceful heartland of the country felt safe and secure. *Heck, bad things happened in other places such as Oklahoma City where a nut like Timothy McVeigh blew up a federal building, but not here.*

However, the news media became a crucial ally. A partnership developed between the media and the investigative team who, depending on the circumstances, relied upon each other for mutual success. When asked by agents to issue a press release, the local papers printed information regarding items for which the investigators were searching. One of these small stories alerted citizens to be on the lookout for several items, including half of a black-and-white-striped T-shirt in the area around Baltic. It was a long shot, for sure, but investigators had exhausted all other avenues for locating this item.

Over breakfast one morning, in the late fall of 1996, Joel Wudel's girlfriend was reading the *Argus Leader* and came across the article.

"Why in the world would the police be looking for half of a black-and-white T-shirt?" she mused aloud to Joel, her natural curiosity piqued by this strange request by authorities.

Joel stopped mid-sip and asked her to repeat what she just read. He shook his head in disbelief and went over to read the article himself. He'd all but forgotten about the scrap of shirt beneath his front seat. With a tremor of unease, he checked his vehicle, and the T-shirt was right where he left it. Joel drove to the police station, all the while speculating as to whether this was the shirt they wanted and why it had such importance.

"When and where did you find this?" an agent asked Joel.

Joel thought back to that day of the funeral and determined he saw it between 1:30 and 2:00 PM on July 29. Although the agent couldn't tell Joel, the significance was that it helped solidify that Piper was abducted prior to that time. He found the shirt a mile southwest of where officers found the other half of the shirt.

When agents examined the shirt found on Highway 115, it matched the piece of T-shirt found by the search team along the Big Sioux River. Bolstered by this find, the *Argus Leader* agreed to publish an article along with photographs of replica items likely associated with the Anderson crimes. This included duct tape, Mace, eye-bolts, wooden dowels, handcuffs, two-inch link chain, and two pictures of the blue tent from different angles. They wanted the public to be on the lookout to help find these items. Citizens had already assisted in locating some vital evidence. Previously, a man found a tire popper after it flattened one of his tires. He turned the popper in to the authorities, but at the time, the sheriff had no knowledge of Anderson or his crimes. So the device was shelved until publicity about Anderson's abductions reached the sheriff. Because of this, the investigators wondered if anyone else had come across a tire popper. So the *Argus Leader* again aided the investigation by releasing more stories, including one asking for help from anyone who may have seen a tire popper, which was described as a piece of metal about five inches long and two inches wide with a sharp, triangular point welded to one end. In nearby Parker, South Dakota, Amy Anderson (no relation) saw the news and flashed back to what had once occurred to her on a dark highway.

Larisa's Demise

THE TWO YEARS prior to Piper's abduction were the gestation period for Anderson moving from fantasizing about rape and torture to physically carrying out a plan. In 1994, before he acquired a Bronco, Anderson drove a maroon Monte Carlo. One day Anderson was behind the wheel, and riding passenger was his longtime friend Glen Walker. As the two cruised through the streets of Sioux Falls, the conversation took a demented turn. Anderson was again in one of his abnormally perverse moods. The long shadows of twilight added to the depravity of his words.

"I want to grab Larisa, tie her up, and rape her. You can join in the fun. Then we'll finish her off and bury her where she'll never be found." Walker, plain-looking and clean-shaven, obediently listened while occasionally nodding his head. Walker also worked at Morrell's and knew Larisa. "Help me do it, and we'll have a good time."

Walker sat silently contemplating the crime while Anderson detailed the plan for carrying out the abduction and rape. Influence. Anderson had that effect on Walker. It was the dominant personality over a passive follower. In the end, Walker agreed to get involved. With an accomplice at his side, Anderson finalized his plot to kidnap the young mother of two and teetered on the edge of an invisible line that once crossed would forever move him from cad to criminal. In the early morning predawn hours of August 27th, Anderson and Walker coasted through the employee parking lot of Morrell's searching for Larisa's minivan, the one she and her husband purchased to accommodate their growing family. Once they found it, Anderson parked near the minivan and proceeded to let the air out of its front tire. The only sound in the deserted lot was the hiss of escaping air. With the vehicle disabled, the next step was to lie in wait where they could observe the minivan until Larisa got off work.

Shortly after 1:00 AM, they heard the soft tap of shoes approaching. Not another soul was in this area of the lot, and only a distant streetlight cast a dim glow onto the row of parked vehicles. She was alone. As Larisa put her key in the door to unlock it, Anderson crept behind her. He grabbed her violently from behind, snarling, "Don't say a word or you're dead." Larisa struggled against his hold, so Anderson threw her to the ground, straddled her body, and held a knife against her neck. Walker rushed over with a roll of duct tape, thrust her hands together, and bound her wrists. The two men hurled her into the trunk. Within seconds, the Monte Carlo disappeared from the lot.

They headed toward a remote location outside of town that Anderson had chosen with great care. In the days leading up to this night, he fantasized obsessively about abducting Larisa and frequently drove to the place where he intended to rape her as a way of living out the rape before it occurred. Before they reached the outskirts of the city, Walker got cold feet.

"Take me home," he demanded. The realization of the consequences of their actions finally sunk in, and Walker was afraid. After a short disagreement, Anderson relented and drove to Walker's house. Having what he wanted, it no longer mattered to Anderson, whose focus was on his unspeakable intentions for Larisa. When Walker got out, Anderson popped the trunk open, pulled

Larisa out, and made her ride in the front with him. After driving to the predetermined spot, Anderson forced Larisa into the backseat, where he proceeded to cut and rip off her clothing.

"I've never been with any man except my husband," Larisa said, likely grasping at anything that might appeal to Anderson's supposed sensibilities. "What's going to happen to me?"

"That depends on you," Anderson said, although it clearly didn't. His plan was set. Over the course of four hours, he raped her repeatedly. Larisa pleaded for her life, saying that she was pregnant and wouldn't tell what he'd just done to her if only he'd let her go. Her terrified reactions delighted Anderson, who relished the total control he exercised over her. His plan was to suffocate Larisa and then revive her over and over to terrorize her, but he changed his mind. After he raped her for the last time, he began slowly taping her mouth and nose shut with duct tape. With a firm grip, he began winding the tape tighter and tighter around her head until her mouth and nose were completely sealed off from oxygen. He purposely left her eyes un-taped so he could look into them as she struggled. When the last shudder of life left her body, he unceremoniously loaded her back into the Monte Carlo and casually went back home for a few hours of sleep. At some point, he decided he wanted a trophy to mark his accomplishment and removed Larisa's necklace, a recent gift from her husband. Anderson decided to get Walker's help in disposing of the body, either because he wanted assistance with the physical labor involved or had a desire to pull Walker deeper into the crime.

When Walker got off work at 4:00 PM, Anderson was in the parking lot waiting for him with Larisa's body in the trunk. Walker approached, and Anderson told him to get in. Although most acquaintances were put off by Anderson's arrogance, his words held a certain power over Walker, who soon found himself headed off into the countryside with Anderson.

"This body can't ever be found," Anderson said with a tone that carried enough urgency to convince Walker he should do whatever Anderson said. They were headed west toward Lake Vermillion. Anderson maneuvered the car down a dirt road that was rarely used as it only led to the base of a remote hill. Not far off the path was a large chokecherry bush with leafy branches spanning over ten feet in diameter. Shielded by the immense bush, they went to work with their shovels. They dug a shallow grave just big enough for Larisa's body, which they pulled beneath the branches before dumping her inside. They thoroughly covered and camouflaged their work, then returned to Sioux Falls. Time rolled on. Falling and drifting snow piled up over the ground where Larisa lay. In spring, heavy rains thickened the vegetation, obscuring the lonely gravesite. Though the seasons changed, hope that Larisa would be found stayed constant in the Dumansky home.

The Dark Highway
November 10, 1994

THE ELATION THAT came from successfully abducting Larisa was short-lived. Although fantasizing about brutal sexual domination had satisfied his cravings in the past, this no longer fulfilled Anderson's obsessive compulsions. He was like an animal that hones its skills with each hunt. His life consisted of relentless urges for another violent sexual act.

A pretty 26-year-old from the small town of Parker, Amy Anderson, no relation to Robert, worked at a Sioux Falls brokerage. Robert Anderson conducted business at the same brokerage. Amy had no idea her path would cross again soon with the devious killer.

Robert was spending a lot of time with a longtime friend, Jamie Hammer, and attempted to get Hammer involved in grabbing women. Although the two friends shared many interests on the surface, the things Anderson wanted to do ran much too deep for Hammer, who wanted no part of the crimes his friend described. Hammer flat out told his longtime companion that he wasn't interested. So Robert Anderson again lured his criminal associate Glen Walker into the next kidnapping. After some persuasion, Walker was game for a night of assault.

On November 10th, Amy was spending time in Sioux Falls with a good friend. The two women finished dining at Minerva's, a popular restaurant, and eventually wound down their evening. They climbed into Amy's car and drove to her apartment in Parker, South Dakota.

Around 9:00 PM, they headed out again to drop off Amy's friend at the farm where she was staying. Dark came early in November, casting the lightly traveled tar road in total blackness. Amy's headlights illuminated glimpses of the picked stubble cornfields along the highway. Following not far behind was the maroon Monte Carlo occupied by Walker and Anderson, who kept a steady pace behind her vehicle. They were prepared with several tire poppers, a knife, duct tape, ether, and handcuffs.

On a secluded section of the highway, a vehicle drove right up to Amy's bumper, and its headlights filled the interior with blinding brightness. She slowed down to let the vehicle pass, which it did, but not before rolling along beside her. The maroon car suddenly accelerated and moved directly in front of Amy's car, then slowed down. Amy signaled to change lanes and passed the maroon car, hoping to put distance between the erratic driver and herself. While passing the car, the two women noted that it was a Monte Carlo and that two males were inside. In a cat-and-mouse game, the Monte Carlo passed Amy and once again slowed to a near stop in her path.

The women became uneasy and annoyed with the other vehicle. Amy tried slowing her vehicle to a crawl in hopes that the Monte Carlo would drive away. It worked. The other vehicle sped to the crest of an approaching hill and vanished from sight to the relief of the two women, who proceeded down the highway.

Suddenly, Amy's car struck something which clanged and bounced along the undercarriage with metallic thuds. It didn't seem significant, so they drove on. A few minutes later, Amy pulled into her friend's driveway. They checked over the car and noted that one tire was slowly leaking air. The closest place to fix the tire was at a service station a few miles away back in Tea. Amy thought she could make it there, so the two quickly said their goodbyes, and Amy headed east.

She only made it a mile or two down the tar road before the car began handling poorly and became difficult to steer, indicating that she wasn't going to make it to the air hose. In frustration, she pulled onto the shoulder, killed the ignition, exited the car, and popped open the trunk. She was about to reach into the trunk when a car approached, passing her disabled vehicle, then pulled a U-turn and returned to park near her on the opposite side of the road.

It was the maroon Monte Carlo.

A chubby man about 5'9" with facial hair and wearing a dark jacket and baseball cap approached her. He didn't say anything, but Amy assumed he was a Good Samaritan even though the maroon car tailgated her earlier. "Thanks for stopping!" she said and showed the man where the jack was.

He reached into the trunk for a moment but then withdrew his hand. Amy then leaned in to grab the jack and was stunned when the man lurched forward and clutched her tightly around the waist. He heaved and tried to drag her away from her vehicle. Amy was terrified but somehow had the composure to fight back. She screamed, shoved and twisted, and gripped the car with one hand.

Her act of desperation knocked Robert Anderson off balance, and his hands broke loose from her waist. The momentum caused him to stumble backward. Amy seized the brief seconds of opportunity and sprinted away into the dark night, staying as best she could on the highway, not wanting to stumble and fall into the ditch where she'd be vulnerable.

Each second stretched into a frightening time-warp. She hadn't run far when headlights appeared in the distance. As if a prayer was answered, Amy ran toward the lights, shouting and waving her arms in the path of the car headed toward her. "Let's get out of here," she heard one of the men yell while the oncoming car slowed to avoid hitting her. The two wide-eyed occupants willingly let Amy in. They were teenagers, and all three women watched as two men hustled into the Monte Carlo and peeled off, heading west.

The teenagers whisked Amy to the Tea service station, where they immediately called 911. The local authorities pursued her report, but without a license number and only a basic description of the suspects, there wasn't much they could do. Fear spread around the area when people heard what happened to her, but as weeks passed, the magnitude of what occurred began to fade.

Altered Plans

ANDERSON TRIED THE tire poppers five times, but the devices never got him a female. After the botched attempt to kidnap Amy which resulted in two eyewitnesses who might be able to identify him or his car, Anderson modified his tactics. He mulled over the idea of getting rid of the tire poppers yet held on to them in case. There was a sense of deep pride in the macabre devices he'd created. He altered his car by installing a custom switch that turned off the headlights, taillights, and brake lights so the vehicle couldn't be seen in the dark.

The system of physically wrestling a woman into his vehicle, even with an accomplice, opened the door for an escape. Then Walker added an unexpected challenge to Anderson's plans. Walker was so unnerved by the struggle on the highway he announced he "was out" for good. It was a snub Anderson would never forget or forgive despite their nearly lifelong friendship. Walker and Anderson parted ways in a cloud of bitterness. In fact, Anderson's anger later fueled a plot to have Walker murdered.

Now without a partner, Anderson decided the knife no longer yielded enough power. He needed more control. He needed to use his firearm. He again started spending more time with his close friend, Jamie Hammer, whom Anderson still believed he could talk into helping with an abduction. The two would drive out by Lake Vermillion to practice with the 9mm handgun to pass the time. Anderson invariably turned the conversations to perverse sex and the domination of women. Each time he was with Hammer, Anderson moved closer to revealing his final plan. In a method similar to getting used to cold water bit by bit, he then tried to lure Hammer into his lair. Anderson attempted to create excitement and interest by discussing a variety of ways to seize a victim and sexually assault her.

But it didn't take long for Hammer to again put a damper on Anderson's conspiracy. Hammer was accustomed to doing what he wanted when he wanted and made it clear he had no interest in following through with this criminal scheme. However, this setback did not discourage Anderson. His insatiable desire for devious sexual acts intensified his creative ideas on how to successfully abduct, rape, torture, and kill any woman of his choosing. He continued playing out various strategies to ensure a successful and airtight plan. He became more proficient with the pistol. His desire for a violent encounter was so overpowering that he started going to the chokecherry bush where Larisa was buried to relive the act of killing her. He'd pull out his handgun and fire several rounds into the dirt that covered her body, all the while fantasizing and recreating in his mind the way he felt that early morning so many months ago when she took her last breath. The act excited and temporarily fulfilled him.

When he was finished, he would drive down the isolated gravel road past a trailer house with wooden pews in the yard and where he sometimes saw a pretty and petite woman outside. Anderson began obsessing over Piper's legs, which had caught his attention. He had to have her, and he'd do it on his own.

Playing the Game
and Covering His Tracks
Thursday, July 25
and Friday, July 26, 1996

LIKE A NAGGING burr, a bothersome thought occasionally reoccurred to Anderson. Since his friendship with Walker had started to unravel, Anderson felt forced to act. His concern was due to his former accomplice being the only other person who knew where Larisa's remains lay buried. If Walker got pinched for a crime, he could chirp information about Larisa's grave to gain a reduced or dismissed sentence. Like a savvy chess player, Anderson decided to make a move that would leave Walker unable to counter. Anderson would make sure he could never be arrested for Larisa's murder, and the way to do this was to get rid of her remains from under the chokecherry bush. Once this was accomplished, he would scatter her parts where they would never be found.

Anderson had sold his Monte Carlo and now owned a vehicle more conducive to carrying out his criminal activities. Under the shroud of darkness, he rattled down the dusty trail near Lake Vermillion in his Ford Bronco and stopped near the enormous bush. The black night was broken by the click of a flashlight, its beam illuminating the large shrub and casting long, irregular shadows onto the tall grasses beyond. Under this artificial light, he used a folding camp shovel for the grisly task. Anderson removed the topsoil and uncovered Larisa's skeletal remains. Using the sharp blade of the shovel, he began dismembering the bones into manageable sections. He tediously broke each tooth from the skull to prevent dental records from being used to identify the remains, then piled her bones together and put them inside the vehicle. He replaced the dirt and smoothed it over to make the grave inconspicuous. Driving around the countryside, Anderson threw pieces of the skeleton into the river, down ravines, and into overgrown ditches until the final piece was discarded. If Walker ever ratted him out, investigators would go to the chokecherry bush and find nothing. Walker would look like a desperate liar. Months or years from now, no one, not even Anderson, would be able to find the bones that sunk to the river bottom or became covered by weeds and thorns. It was, like most of his plans, botched.

Piper's Abduction
Monday, July 29, 1996

ANDERSON WAS OBSESSED with thoughts of violently raping the pretty, young woman he saw gathering the mail outside her trailer house. It was her legs that caught and kept his attention. Brutal images of overpowering the woman played out incessantly in his mind. The previous Friday when he'd planned to abduct and rape her, he was foiled by her husband coming to the door. He had to be more prepared, so this time he came armed with his 9mm pistol and would not be denied this person he desired to possess. If the husband was there again, he'd shoot and kill him.

It was the morning of Monday, July 29, when Anderson steered his vehicle into the driveway of the Streyle home. He knocked at the front door, and a little girl opened it.

"Where's your mom?"

The little girl pointed to a back room. With his pistol drawn, Anderson rushed in and met Piper coming down the hallway. At first, Piper stared at him, frozen in fear, while he shouted for her to lie down on her stomach. She wouldn't do it. Anderson shoved her back, and she landed in the children's bedroom as he charged toward her. Piper grabbed for his gun, and in the struggle, it went off, sending a resonating blast through the home. Later, it would be debated whether the handgun's discharge was by accident or was a warning shot. Piper still fought on, but Anderson forced her to her stomach and cuffed her hands. She screamed for Shaina and Nathan to run and hide. He quickly overpowered Piper and shackled her ankles, then with the gun leveled at her, he demanded to know where the slip of paper was on which he'd written his name and address the other day. Piper told him, and he retrieved the note. Barefoot and wearing only underwear and a black-and-white nightshirt, Piper was carried from the house while she kicked and screamed. The woman whose husband referred to her as the most photogenic yet godly woman he knew was furiously fighting for her life on a gravel driveway while her two young children huddled with fear inside their home. Anderson threatened her with the pistol, then fired it to show he meant business. The semi-automatic spit the casing into the driveway, but Anderson could not locate it and was in a hurry to get away. He pushed Piper into the passenger's seat and sped off.

With the threat of the pistol, Piper sat immobile, helpless against the handcuffs binding her wrists and ankles. Anticipating what was ahead, Piper tried appealing to his emotions.

"I'm menstruating," she said evenly.

"I don't care about that," Anderson said.

"My husband's the only man I've been with."

Instead of going down the road to Lake Vermillion where he buried Larisa, he headed in the opposite direction. There are nearly forty miles between the Streyle home and Anderson's secret destination, creating a terrifying ride for Piper. He brought her to a place along the Big Sioux River where the thick brush and mature trees dominated the banks and blocked out the sunlight. Heavy shadows created the illusion of perpetual twilight. Anderson parked, turned off the ignition, and went to the rear of the vehicle to prepare the bondage board.

...Can and Will Be Used Against You
August 2, 12:30 AM

INVESTIGATORS WERE NOW armed with Anderson's statement, Shaina's identification of Anderson as the mean man who carried off her mommy, and an explanation of why his blue Bronco was described as black with black wheels. It wasn't much, but the evidence was enough to connect 26-year-old Anderson to the abduction of Piper. On August 2nd, just after midnight, a warrant was issued for his arrest. At 1:30 AM, DCI agents went into the John Morrell packing house where Anderson was working. A supervisor led the agents to their suspect, who was wearing work clothes, cowboy boots, and a Camel cigarette baseball cap. Without incident he was read his rights, and his hands were cuffed behind his back. The charge was for the first-degree kidnapping of Piper Streyle. The man who obtained so much enjoyment handcuffing his victims, now had the tables turned. News of the arrest spread through the packing house like a fanned grassfire, with wildly speculative guesses as to why he was taken away by detectives. A stunned Anderson was placed in an isolation cell for his own protection. Bail was set at $500,000, which he was never able to raise. Unbeknownst to Anderson, his feet would not see the streets of freedom again.

Word of Anderson's arrest hit the local news circuit with *Argus Leader* headlines reading *Robert Anderson Arrested in Abduction, Suspect Went to Streyle House on Day of Abduction* and *Streyle's Husband Thrilled*. Like many criminal sociopaths, Anderson was able to lead a double life completely hidden from family, friends, and coworkers. Shortly after his arrest, Anderson's wife, Elaine, stood by her man. Chain-smoking Misty cigarettes, she spoke with the media:

"This is part about the bad times in one's life. He's innocent. His eyes tell it all. The authorities want someone so bad that they are just going after one person. Robert is scared, and we both cried. He didn't kidnap anyone," Elaine stated emphatically. She offered up an excuse for her husband, claiming he was out at the Streyle house because of her desire to enroll their children in a church camp. It was an improbable story that had the opposite effect and made it appear that Anderson didn't even have a single alibi. While Elaine worked the day shift at Morrell's, a neighbor took care of their three children, ages 5, 3, and 1. Anderson had another son from his first marriage but hadn't seen the boy for three years. Elaine explained it away by professing that her husband loved this son so much that he didn't want the boy to be in the middle of a fight so chose not to see him.

She did her best to portray him in a positive light. In jail he read technical engineering magazines and had plans to build his own car. He had hobbies and enjoyed playing video games and collecting comic books. In fact, his collection expanded to the point that Elaine insisted he stop buying them despite his knack for being able to predict which comic books would grow in value. He decided to try his hand at the stock market instead and discovered he had similar luck choosing stocks of good value. She repeatedly declared his innocence and his love of family. Interestingly, Anderson's own father would only comment that he hadn't spoken to his son for a very long time and didn't want to start talking about him now.

A neighbor originally informed the police that Anderson's Bronco was painted black. A few days later he withdrew the statement and came to Anderson's defense.

"I called it black in my statement. I really don't know why I called it black. It has never been black."

But Anderson's sneaky attempt to disguise his vehicle backfired on him. With everything but the headlights painted black, the Bronco stood out awkwardly.

Then the neighbor suggested that someone likely kidnapped Piper before Anderson showed up. So, when Shaina saw Anderson, she wrongly assumed he was the one who took her mother. The neighbor's unlikely defense demonstrated the extent to which Anderson had deceived those around him and hidden his double life.

Larisa's husband, Bill, told of a different Anderson, the man he knew when the two worked in the same department at Morrell's in 1991-92. Bill recalled how Anderson enjoyed talking about "sex and the way he performs it, and all that dirty stuff." He remembered Anderson as being "nasty and dirty-minded." In the days following, other Morrell employees reported having seen Anderson with pornographic pictures in his work locker, including nude photos of a family member.

Vance provided a statement to the press expressing that he was "thrilled" at Anderson's arrest.

In an interview from jail, although Anderson's voice was unsteady, he said that other inmates questioned him regarding how he managed to stay so calm. He remarked that he was busy reading the Bible, a lie that seemed to go together with the claim that he stopped at the Streyles' to inquire about their Prairie View Bible Camp. He continued to profess that he was in the "wrong place at the wrong time."

Metamorphosis of Justice

THE METHODICAL SOUND of the printing press banged and clattered like a roaring freight train. This newspaper office in remote Martin, South Dakota, was where Larry Long spent much of his time. It was here that he learned how to operate the machines that spat out a stack of papers to provide the surrounding townsfolk with the latest news. While many local children would recall a childhood filled with the scent of hayfields or cattle barns, Larry's was that of strong, black coffee mixed with the chemical acridness of printing ink.

"Larry, run down to the station and buy a gallon a white gas. Hurry back," his father might yell over the clanging of the loud machinery. It was a chore not suitable for a very young child and one that filled Larry with pride knowing he was now old enough to be entrusted with some of the potent substances required in the print shop, such as the white gas to burn off tape from the printing casts. He watched his parents put in excruciatingly long hours with nary a vacation since the news never took a break. When not in school, a day of work for Larry would begin with the first rays of morning light and not wind down until twilight. His family ran the *Bennett County Booster II* newspaper; the II came about because years prior his grandmother operated the *Bennett County Booster* while homesteading in 1912. The town is situated near two Indian Reservations, Rosebud and Pine Ridge. It's an often-forgotten expanse of rolling grasslands dotted with colorful wildflowers and deep-carved ravines with pine thickets ideal for the abundant deer population. In the open areas, pronghorn antelope out-sprint hungry coyotes, but the bitter winters that sweep across the prairie send all the wildlife struggling to survive. It was in this environment that Long's value system developed from the strong Christian influence of not only his parents but also his grandmother. In her younger days as a single, female homesteader, she believed it her duty to attend church every Sunday, although no church existed anywhere near her tiny cabin. So, on the Lord's Day, she would mount her horse for the challenging eight-mile ride to the closest church, one that was run by a tribal lay minister. She meditated silently throughout the service since she didn't understand a word, as it was conducted in the Lakota language. When the service ended, she mounted her horse for the long ride back home.

As a child, Larry and his younger sister spent many evenings at their grandmother's house listening to Bible stories while their parents worked into the night to put out a paper. And so, he developed a solid philosophy of right and wrong. When he finally headed off to college, he knew one thing he did not want to pursue was a job in the newspaper business. What he didn't know was that his career choices would lead him to a starring role in one of the state's biggest criminal trials.

After completing undergraduate work at SDSU, Long graduated from USD Law School in 1972 and briefly served in the U.S. Army. After his discharge, he returned home and began his law career. 1973 saw the area around Martin turn from cattle country into a war zone when many Native Americans who held to their traditional beliefs clashed with leaders of the Bureau of Indian Affairs, or BIA. These Natives felt the BIA on the Pine Ridge Indian Reservation had failed to feed and house the people. The feud escalated, turning bloody with drive-by shootings and violence on both sides. The anti-BIA leaders felt they needed help and contacted the American Indian Movement (AIM). A caravan of over 200 vehicles filled with AIM members and armed with assault rifles, handguns, and high-powered hunting rifles rolled toward Pine Ridge to support the traditional belief faction in this struggle for control. AIM came in not only to help but to draw attention to their belief that the United States, acting through the BIA, was ignoring the needs of Native Americans and treaty rights. The presence of AIM caused dissention, as many of the Oglala Sioux were opposed to violence and the way AIM operated. Most of the country remained largely unaware of the problems on Pine Ridge even though over a span of three years there were 64 unsolved Native American murders and an accumulation of 1,200 arrests. AIM took over by force the small town of Wounded Knee, 35 miles west of Martin, resulting in Governor Richard Kneip calling in National Guard troops. Before the revolt was contained, more Native Americans lost their lives and two FBI agents were murdered. Against this backdrop, Long was appointed State's Attorney for Bennett County in March 1973.

His career advanced, and in 1991, he became Deputy Attorney General working out of Pierre, South Dakota. One day Attorney General Mark Barnett summoned Long to his office and presented him with a job assignment unusual for Long's position.

"We received a call from McCook County prosecutor Roger Gerlach. They have a high-profile case and need our assistance," Mark explained. This was typical of prosecutors from small counties to request help from the attorney general's office as they were not equipped with staff for unexpected large cases. "We're also short-staffed, and I need you to handle this case," Mark said, giving Long a binder of paperwork. Long returned to his office and began perusing the files for the case against Robert Leroy Anderson.

Facing the Music

IT WAS A single charge of first-degree kidnapping and carried a maximum sentence of life in prison. At the arraignment, one of Anderson's lawyers questioned why officers brought his client into the courtroom in handcuffs and foot restraints. He complained that this had the effect of making Anderson look guilty. It was one of the first of many trivial defenses Anderson's dream team of lawyers would use to point to his innocence. It is commonly said in many states that a good portion of death row inmates are there due to inadequate representation in court. Consequently, years of appeals follow from prisoners claiming they were poorly defended. To prevent this, the state of South Dakota takes the opposite route and attempts to provide the best lawyers from the start to a defendant charged with a capital crime. Therefore, because Anderson was unable to pay for his own defense, he was assigned two of the most highly sought-after lawyers in the state: Sid Strange and Mike Unke. It was an A team of seasoned veterans with distinguished histories of representing their clients. Those from the legal field considered this a formidable match for the prosecution team, which was not only accomplished but well-respected also. Deputy Attorney General Larry Long, Attorney General Mark Barnett, and Assistant Attorney General Patty Froning geared up for an intensive trial. Gerlach, the state's attorney for McCook County, had already completed the initial proceedings.

Months before, when prosecutor Larry Long was first handed the binder of evidence against Anderson, the case was mostly based on circumstantial evidence and Shaina's identification of Anderson as "the mean man" who carried her mother away. Since then, he and the other prosecutors strengthened the case with critical forensic evidence, yet he was realistic enough to acknowledge the generous loopholes that the defense would surely exploit. Yes, Anderson painted his Bronco, but the defense could argue that this was done so he could see how the washable black color looked on his SUV. Anderson's lawyers could contend that there was no way one bottle of tempera paint would be enough to cover a vehicle. At the crime lab, Mike Daugherty and Rex Riis borrowed a Bronco, and using a three-inch paintbrush and a bucket, diluted the liquid black paint with water. It took them twenty-three minutes to paint the entire vehicle black, including the rims and chrome. After it dried, it took seven minutes to remove the paint at a carwash. There was one problem. It was pointed out that Anderson's Bronco had an unusual pattern painted on the side. They located a Bronco similar in color to Anderson's and recreated the custom interwoven design from his vehicle by using masking tape. Having accomplished that, they painted the vehicle again with the tempera paint and videotaped the process to show the jury. It proved the Bronco could be fully painted and washed clean in a short amount of time.

The prosecution had to predict other arguments the defense would likely raise. Yes, they would say, Anderson stopped at the Streyle home to ask about the Bible Camp, but so had others. The Streyles encouraged people to seek out their ministry. None of this meant that Anderson was responsible for any crime. The reason for not seeking a murder charge was clear. There was no body. The defense objected to a kidnapping trial without a body and noted that they couldn't recall such a thing happening before in the state of South Dakota. Countering this, the prosecution cited legal proof that the law was on their side with this, and that finding a body is not required to prove kidnapping or murder. Long and his team decided to pursue only a kidnapping charge, since it would leave the door open to try Anderson for murder later should more evidence or a body be found. Since murder is a different charge than kidnapping, it would not be a violation of double jeopardy, which prohibits an accused person from being tried for the same crime twice.

Prior to the start of the trial, the defense continued to throw up blockades that could hinder the case. Each attack had to be addressed thoroughly. One attorney claimed that Anderson wasn't read his rights before the first interrogation, which would render the interview inadmissible in court. If agreed to by the judge, it would deal a heavy blow to the prosecution, because they would lose the ability to present the evidence they collected as a result of the interview. Testimony on suppressing the interview was intense and left both sides anxious. It took several court dates to hammer out the details. Finally, Judge Boyd McMurchie ruled that only the first hour of Anderson's interview was admissible but not the last six and a half hours, since about one hour into the interview, Anderson asked to talk to a lawyer and go home. While far from ideal, the prosecution rejoiced. The first hour when Anderson admitted being at the Streyles' and changed his story several times was the most critical part of the interview.

But vital evidence was suppressed. The defense argued to keep out testimony from Amy regarding her near abduction as well as information about a 17-year-old girl who was restrained with handcuffs by Robert Anderson. This was determined to be testimony about his character rather than directly related to the case at hand so therefore was not admissible. "That is a separate and unique crime," the defense lawyers argued, adding that such testimony could prejudice the jurors against Anderson.

Anderson's disturbing tire poppers also became objects of contention. The defense argued that the tire poppers should be disregarded as evidence since they were not used in the kidnapping of Piper Streyle. Even though the judge ultimately ruled that the evidence of the tire poppers was inadmissible, there was no denying that these creations were designed to assist Anderson in his evil plans. If the prosecution would have been allowed to use all the information they had about Anderson's tire poppers, it would have been a big strike against his defense team. Anderson had parts of these devices in his locker at Morrell's. Three motorists, including Amy, were prepared to testify that they ran over the tire poppers. But their evidence would not be heard in the kidnapping trial.

The weight of the case relied on the only witness to the kidnapping, a three-and-a-half-year-old girl, and her testimony. Although Shaina picked Anderson out of the photo lineup, there was understandable doubt that she would do the same thing in the courtroom. Anderson's lawyers filed a motion to prevent Shaina from testifying based on her age, and this was something the judge had to consider. During the hearing to determine Shaina's competence to testify, the defense prepared 124 questions with which to grill the young girl.

THE TRIAL PLAYED out behind a heavy layer of security for which officials spent months preparing. They chose the third-floor courtroom of Aberdeen, South Dakota's much smaller City Hall rather than the large courthouse which would have required securing more area. Security was provided around the clock. Five locks were added to various doors in the building, and one entrance was temporarily blocked so that there was only one way in. Then a metal detector was set up at the only entrance to the third floor. The hatred toward Anderson made him a security risk. There was a distinct possibility that a vigilante could try to attack him in some way, and authorities took this potential threat seriously. All the precautions proved necessary when a frenzy of people wanted in to watch the trials. So much so that a ticket system was developed with different-colored passes for family members, the media, jurors, and the handful of spectators fortunate enough to procure a ticket.

THE TRIAL BEGAN on April 8, 1997, with Judge Boyd McMurchie presiding. McMurchie ruled that when the time came for Shaina to testify, it would be from a room at the local library, since the priority was to keep her from having to see Anderson. The room at the library would become the courtroom. Anderson and others would see Shaina's testimony over the state's Rural Development Television Network. Shaina was appointed an attorney to watch over her welfare during the proceedings as well as a child therapist, Dr. Cynthia Pilkington, to work with her due to the traumatic nature of the testimony. Pilkington explained that Shaina had not recovered and still experienced bad dreams and guilt. Shaina blamed herself for being the one to let the bad man in the house. Without her testimony, they could only show that Anderson was suspicious and in the vicinity of the crime scene. To bolster their case, prosecutors sought out DNA evidence from the four strands of hair found on the bondage board in the Bronco as well as the mass of hair found on the duct tape along the river. DNA from the roots of two of the hairs found on Anderson's bondage board matched DNA from blood on the menstrual pads from the Streyles' trash can. The use of DNA evidence was new, and many people were still skeptical of its legitimacy. The prosecution could only hope that the testimony of the forensic experts would be powerful enough to persuade the jury.

As an unexpected bonus, Anderson's friend Jamie Hammer agreed to testify for the prosecution. At first Hammer refused. Based on numerous run-ins with the law, he had little faith in the legal system and was concerned that any information he gave might be turned back on him. Although he had not committed any crimes with Anderson, he thought the investigators might come up with creative ways to tie him to his friend's wrongdoings. When the prosecution offered him limited immunity for his testimony, should he say something to incriminate himself, Hammer agreed.

He was prepared to give details about Anderson's obsession with stalking women and the plans to kidnap them. Hammer was concerned with the possibility that his former friend could concoct a story to place blame on Hammer. Headstrong, he was not an amateur at dealing with legal affairs. He purchased a tape recorder and had it rolling during every interview he sat through regardless if he were talking to a DCI agent, attorney, or anyone else who wanted his information. He followed his lawyer's advice and kept every tape he recorded. While Hammer didn't believe he committed a crime, he wasn't going to leave anything to chance in case he misspoke, or his words were misconstrued. The authorities knew that Hammer's information would be a significant part of nailing Anderson and had no reason to think Hammer was involved in the kidnapping. Hammer had an alibi. He was at work all day on July 29, 1996.

There were obvious problems in using Hammer as a witness as is often the case in criminal testimony. People who associate with criminals tend to have questionable backgrounds themselves, and this fact is used by the other side to discredit their testimony. There is a saying among trial lawyers that one needs to "take sandpaper to a witness and clean him up," which was what Long was prepared to do. Then, with the best-laid plans, Hammer threw a wrench into everything by getting arrested two weeks before Anderson's trial. When Long investigated the charges, he shook his head and pictured the testimony of his witness going up in smoke. "You've got to be kidding," Long said aloud.

"THIS IS A kidnapping trial. With a show of hands, have any of you, or anyone you know, been the victim of a kidnapping?"

No hands went up.

"Now a more sensitive question. Have any of you been a victim of a sexual assault? If you raise your hand, we can talk privately." The prosecutor paused, and a few hands went up. It was important information attorneys needed to know about the group of potential jurors. Selecting the right jurors is an art form for attorneys and being good at it can spell success. The wrong jury panel can mean a lot of intense hard work ends in defeat for the prosecution or defense team. There is no set formula on picking a jury that is taught in law school. Many times, it comes down to good gut instinct combined with experience. A continued barrage of questions was asked of the jury pool, and based on what was discovered, the attorneys focused on citizens they wanted to see as jurors and those people they wanted eliminated from this case.

Long was looking for people with specific traits such as a strong value system and a sense of family structure. He wanted someone raised in a loving home by quality parents and who was level-headed without a history of arrests and therefore no ax to grind against the court system. He leaned toward choosing females as they were more inclined to relate to the horrors of Piper's experience. A favorable male candidate was someone who could relate to Piper as a daughter, sister, or mother. The defense looked for jurors with excellent common sense. "This is going to consume all your attention," one attorney said, referring to the fact that there would be more technical evidence presented than in any other case during his thirty years in the courtroom.

After six days, the longest jury selection Judge McMurchie could remember, thirteen women and three men were chosen to allow for twelve jurors and four alternates. To ensure that all jurors listened carefully throughout the length of the trial, none of them knew who the four alternates were. The judge would reveal who the twelve jurors were once it came time to deliberate.

ONE OF THE primary concerns of the defense attorneys was Shaina's testimony. They explained to jurors that it could appear they were intimidating or even bullying Shaina, but it was their job to question her. It was the job of the jurors to keep an open mind, and the defense worried that the cross-examination of such a small child would be too emotional for some of them to handle fairly. As the jury selection was in progress, a defense attorney addressed the potential pool of people regarding Shaina.

"You can't make a decision because you feel bad for someone or you feel sympathetic to the plight of a little girl. The final decision has to be based upon the strength of the evidence," the lawyer instructed.

WITNESS JAMIE HAMMER was unpredictable. At times, he spoke first and thought second. Above all, he spoke his mind. Whether or not he might say something that would benefit the defense rather than the prosecution was a serious concern. Nonetheless, the prosecution team believed his testimony was crucial, so they spent a great deal of time preparing Jamie for what was ahead. His extensive criminal record and therefore lack of reliability opened him up to being torn apart by the defense. On top of it all, Hammer got arrested two weeks before trial. He was drinking at his Sioux Falls home and decided to have a pizza delivered. The delivery man was running late, which caused Hammer to lose his temper. He stepped into his driveway holding a sub-machine gun, and when the pizza man pulled up, Hammer let loose with firing a series of rat-a-tat-tats into the air. The gun's action spit a shower of empty brass casings that clanked and bounced off the concrete. The terrified delivery man hightailed it out of the neighborhood and called 911. Hammer was put into custody and charged with reckless discharge of a firearm and possession of a firearm while intoxicated. Authorities confiscated a sub-machine gun, a shotgun, and boxes of ammunition. All these items were off limits for Hammer to possess since he had a prior felony conviction on his record.

If there were any other options, Long would not have risked putting Hammer in front of the jury. Too many things could go wrong. There were too many ways to discredit Hammer and make the prosecution look desperate for a witness. Once Hammer got in front of a jury, no one could have anticipated his haphazard and animated responses.

Shaina

The legal debate continued to rage surrounding the decision to have Shaina testify for the prosecution. The lead defense attorney contended that she was too young, and that his cross-examination would be too rough.

"People are not going to like me after I have to question that child, but it's my job," the attorney argued.

The prosecution also had concerns regarding Shaina being a key witness. The hard line of questioning by the defense could reduce Shaina to tears and cause the little girl to become so upset that she would be unable to testify about her mother's killer. Both sides wondered how she would hold up. Even experts in the area of child development had no pat answers, but one specialist stated that children do sometimes pay better attention to details than adults. It was Child Abuse Prevention month, and people predicted that advocacy groups would be outraged should Shaina be verbally battered in court. The judge questioned Shaina and determined that she was competent enough to know right from wrong and understood the oath. In the end, it was decided that Shaina would testify, and the defense would cross-examine her.

Both sides made their opening statements to set the foundation for the trial. During the two hours it took Long to lay out an overview of the evidence, Piper's mother sobbed softly throughout. Seated across from her were Anderson's wife and mother. As far as physical evidence, the prosecution withheld one key piece until the end of the trial, knowing that it would have a huge emotional impact on the jury.

One witness called to the stand was Tim Beaner, whose father lived near the Streyles. Beaner testified that he and his family drove by the Streyle home twice on July 29th. The first time was about 11:45 AM, and they saw two children in the yard who looked upset. The family didn't stop because there was a car parked next to the trailer, and they assumed there was nothing terribly wrong. After driving to Lake Vermillion, they turned around and went past the Streyles' again about 30 minutes later. This time a black Bronco was parked in the driveway near the road. The children were no longer outside, but a man with a mustache was walking from the house to the Bronco.

On the morning that Shaina was to testify, those associated with the kidnapping trial anxiously pondered how to protect the little girl yet encourage her to answer questions for the jury. Present in a large room at the public library were the jurors, the judge, a court reporter, Shaina's advocate lawyer, reporters, Long, Froning, Sid Strange, and a few spectators that primarily included family members. Wearing a blue and white dress, red tights, and red shoes, Shaina cuddled a doll and sat on the floor with a fluffy security blanket she used during therapy sessions. The therapist had provided Shaina with the blanket to feel safe when talking about the trauma she experienced. If the emotions ran too high, Shaina covered her head with the blanket and crawled beneath it, which signaled she was done answering questions. All those who remained back at the courtroom were glued to the closed-circuit television screen, which showed Shaina sitting on the blanket surrounded by a few toys. The hope was that Shaina would be comfortable with Froning present, as the two had spent some time together. Shaina was sworn in, and the questioning began.

"How old are you?" the judge asked.

Shaina fidgeted and held up four fingers.

"Shaina, can you show me the mean man?" Froning laid out the photo lineup on the floor.

But it was not to be. Shaina pulled the blanket over her head and slowly enveloped herself, shutting out the rest of the world. Tears started to well up in the courtroom. The shape of her tiny, curled up body was visible beneath the fuzzy blanket that grew smaller as Shaina pulled it tightly beneath her. Three more times Froning attempted to get Shaina to tell about the mean man, but she remained cocooned in the safety of her blanket. Those who were parents or grandparents turned away or hung their heads. Audible sobs rippled through the courtroom. The little girl was overwhelmed. There would be no eyewitness testimony. A distinct feeling swept through the courtroom that the case had veered in favor of the defense. Yet no one was disappointed in Shaina. On the contrary, it only confirmed that the little girl had taken on all she could at this point.

Though Shaina didn't answer Froning's questions, the court still had a way to hear her voice, and the result was dispiriting. On the morning Piper was abducted, Vance called home to touch base with his wife, and when she didn't answer, he left a message on the answering machine. While he was hanging up, Shaina picked up the phone, so the machine kept recording.

"I hope he calls again," Shaina is heard saying, and then there are several seconds of silence. "Papa? Papa?" A busy signal is heard along with Shaina whispering, "Please! Please, call back!" After a minute of random banging noises and faint words, the recording ends.

At that point, the courtroom shifted from anguish into numbness. Spectators wept, and the emotional sway on the jury was tremendous after hearing the voice of a frightened, motherless little girl calling desperately for her daddy.

***

LONG HAD TRAINED himself to handle the stress and bumps that accompanied a trial. There wasn't time for him to labor on Shaina not speaking for Froning. His state of mind was that when things didn't go as desired, the team had to quickly reorganize their strategy. In this case, it meant hitting home the importance of their limited but valuable DNA evidence. They briefed the jury with a short lesson about DNA by explaining that every human's DNA is different except for that of identical twins. DNA can be obtained from blood, bodily fluid, hair roots, and other body parts. The hairs found on the wad of duct tape was too decomposed from being exposed to rain and heat. However, the four human hairs found on the bondage board had been discovered quickly and were in excellent shape. Long cradled a folder under his arm while summarizing the scientific results. Two of the four human hairs from the bondage board in the back of the Bronco were compared to two blood samples from the menstrual pads discovered in the trash can of the Streyles' bathroom. These were evaluated by Cellmark Diagnostics, who had analyzed evidence in both the O.J. Simpson and JonBenet Ramsey cases. This lab was considered the best at extracting and testing DNA. On the stand, forensics expert Anjali Swienton told the jury, "We can say it is one-hundred-million-to-one odds that these hairs came from Piper Streyle than from a random, unrelated female." In other words, the hair would be found in only one out of 100 million Caucasians. Since at the time there were about 112 million white females in the United

States, the expert concluded that the hair could only come from one white female in the entire country, Piper Streyle.

During cross-examination, the defense argued that such a tiny bit of DNA hair root evidence couldn't produce accurate results. But the prosecution's witness, microbiologist Melisa Weber from Cellmark, did such a convincing job of explaining the testing process that one of Anderson's attorneys cut her off mid-sentence in hopes of preventing her from further strengthening the prosecution's case. In desperation, he switched tactics and instead attacked the way the evidence was gathered and handled. He did this since DNA evidence was still gaining credibility as a forensic tool, having only been used in court for about a decade. One tactic for defense lawyers was to question how evidence was gathered since it was difficult to argue the statistical odds of the DNA results.

It was also determined that the animal hairs found on the brown jersey gloves from Anderson's Bronco were dog hairs identical to samples taken from the Streyles' yellow Labrador, Chase. The question was never answered as to whether the dog hairs were picked up randomly or if he petted Chase in the process of the crime.

Another crucial piece of evidence was the scrap of black-and-white cotton cloth found by the state crime lab on the bondage board. The scrap matched Piper's nightshirt.

Though authorities had not located Anderson's pistol, the jury was made aware that two coworkers witnessed him firing a 9mm handgun and that he target practiced at a shooting range near Lake Vermillion. Investigators collected twelve spent 9mm bullet casings from this shooting range. When state ballistics expert Michael Daugherty took the stand, he testified that eleven of the twelve shell casings found at the shooting range came from the same 9mm pistol and matched the shell casing found in the Streyles' driveway. When a gun is fired, it leaves an indentation with distinct firing pin marks. Thus, eleven of the shooting range shell casings and the shell casing from the Streyles' driveway had been fired from the same pistol.

"There is only one gun that could have produced those same marks," Daugherty said. "I do not believe any other gun could have."

Although the defense lawyers grilled almost every witness for the prosecution, Daugherty's evidence was so concrete, that when it came time to cross-examine him, the defense simple stated, "We have no questions, your honor." The jury perhaps breathed a sigh of relief. The trial had entered its fifth week, and the jurors were finding it increasingly difficult to remain focused.

The next evidence was from the sanitary pads taken from the Streyles' bathroom on the day Piper went missing. Cellmark Diagnostics compared blood from the pads to the mixed bloodstain near the crotch of Anderson's blue jeans. A mixed stain contains DNA from more than one person. Anderson's DNA was present because the jeans were his. Blood samples taken from Anderson's wife and children were not a match for this stain. Long summarized the connection to the jury. "Piper was menstruating the day Anderson kidnapped her. It was observed that Anderson did not wear underwear. Piper's blood was found on the inside of Anderson's blue jeans with the obvious conclusion that he raped her."

The forensics expert's conclusion about the bloodstain was not as overwhelming as the evidence from the human hairs since the blood on the blue jeans came from a mixed stain. "We can say that it is 26,000 times more likely that the blood on the jeans came from Piper Streyle than from a random, unrelated female."

The defense countered with the fact that after Anderson's Bronco was searched, it sat overnight unattended in the police parking lot. Someone could have planted evidence in the vehicle to frame Anderson. After all, he associated with several shady people, any one of whom could be the true perpetrator. When it was the prosecution's turn, they responded with the fact that the Bronco only sat unprotected one night before being put on a trailer and hauled to the state crime lab in Pierre, South Dakota. In addition, the four hairs from the bondage board and many other items had already been removed, inventoried, and photographed.

Then came the climactic piece of final evidence. The bondage board. It was a heavy, carpeted board with metal rings in two of the corners to which handcuffs could be attached. When it was hauled in, a sense of anguish overcame the courtroom. The mere presence of the board came to life in a way more powerful than words alone. The horrors that were committed on it became visibly evident with every description of Anderson's unspeakable crimes. The sturdy square of wood dealt a final blow in Anderson's weak defense. The prosecution then requested that jurors be allowed to see the Bronco from which the bondage board was removed in hopes that this would help them visualize where evidence was found. The judge, however, denied this and added that the state's case was very thorough, and therefore nothing new would be gained from viewing the Bronco.

Revenge

WHEN THE DETAILS of what Anderson did to Piper were exposed at the trial, it didn't take long for word to hit the street. The news sent waves of revulsion, anger, and even revenge circulating through the nearby towns. In coffee shops, snippets of talk and gossip acknowledged the hatred and disgust. *Someone ought to do to him just what he did to that young woman,* and *I'd like to have some time alone with that creep and give him what he deserves* were often-echoed sentiments largely met with agreement even by those who'd never met Piper.

To imagine the emotions felt by those close to Piper was unfathomable. For Piper's father, John Potts, the grief and rage nearly pushed him over the edge. He drove hundreds of miles from Rio Medina, Texas, to attend the trial of the man who murdered his daughter. During the jury selection, he extended his arm as if holding an invisible pistol and used his trigger finger to simulate the act of shooting Anderson repeatedly. One day he brought in a small handheld mirror and positioned himself near a window, using it to catch the sun's rays, which he deflected into Anderson's eyes. This was the tipping point that forced courtroom security guards to bring Potts's actions to the attention of Long and Attorney General Mark Barnett. During a court recess, Long and Barnett took Potts aside to discuss what happened.

"You're not going after the death penalty. Since you guys won't kill him, I will," Potts explained in a level voice.

"Take it back," Barnett warned him. "Take it back right now, and tell me you didn't mean it."

"I mean it. I'm going to kill him," Potts said in the same matter-of-fact voice.

"Look, I'm the attorney general and as such am required by law to report your statement to the judge if you said it with serious intentions." He gave this offer with the understanding that Potts was under extreme duress and perhaps needed to cool off. But that was not the case.

"Go ahead. Do what you have to do, but I mean it."

Barnett promptly reported the situation to Judge McMurchie and the defense counsel.

When the judge questioned Potts, the results did not change.

"In my opinion, he needs to die. I'm going to kill him," Potts explained.

The judge's first concern was the safety of everyone at the courthouse. He developed a plan that took into consideration Potts's emotional pain.

"Mr. Potts, you are hereby banished from within one block of the courthouse for as long as the trial lasts. There's a restaurant in your hotel. Every morning you will go to the restaurant and have coffee with a DCI agent. The agent will call this courthouse and confirm that you are at breakfast. Then, and only then, will we move Anderson from the jail to the courthouse. At the conclusion of the day's trial, a DCI agent will again meet you in the eating area of your hotel and confirm to us that you are there. That is when Anderson will be transported back to jail for the night."

For the duration of the trial, Potts obeyed the judge's instructions. From that point on, Anderson was provided a bulletproof vest. The pain displayed by Piper's father symbolized the emotional toll the crimes took on the family members of the victims.

***

NEXT IT WAS time to put Hammer on the stand. Before doing this, and during opening statements, Long made the strategic move of presenting Hammer's background in an honest light by openly acknowledging his dubious past as though he wasn't afraid to have the information out there. Even though he was. If he didn't bring it to light, the defense surely would. This blatant honesty had the effect of softening and minimizing Hammer's grim background. Long's presentation made it clear that the prosecution was open and honest and had nothing to hide.

After approaching the jury, Long moved deliberately in a sweeping side-to-side pattern. Using a confident and direct tone, he addressed them.

"I'm going to tell you that Mr. Hammer does not come to us with a clean background. He has a criminal record and has served time in prison. Mr. Hammer has received treatment for mental health issues, and he has gone through alcohol rehabilitation. He has not always made the best choices, and one of those choices recently got him arrested. But I will tell you that Jamie Hammer made the right choice by refusing to get involved with Robert Anderson's crimes, and he will tell you the truth about what he knows in regard to those horrible crimes," Long concluded.

Hammer was sworn in. He took his seat in the witness box and the eyes of the jurors fell on him. Hammer was rather handsome, with a roughcast, chiseled face that reflected a "been around the block" appearance.

As anticipated, the defense immediately attacked Hammer's character.

"Is it true, Mr. Hammer, you were arrested in Sioux Falls, South Dakota, on March 19, 1997, for discharging a firearm within the city limits of Sioux Falls, South Dakota?"

"Yes," Hammer answered. The defense held its collective breath, knowing that Hammer's next few responses would determine whether the jury considered him credible or not.

"And they took from you two ammo magazines for a .45 caliber Thompson rifle?"

"Correct."

"And didn't the police recover five .45 spent brass shell casings from your driveway?"

Long tightened inside, unable to predict what this unpredictable witness might say.

A look of puzzlement crossed Hammer's face. "They only found five?" he scoffed. "There was more than that!" he responded in a genuinely miffed voice. "They should have found a lot more than that."

After a stunned silence, chuckles rose from the jury box. Hammer was basking in being the center of focus in this intense legal drama. The defense recovered from his unexpected answer and continued. "And didn't the police find a plastic box of 100 Federal high-powered .22 caliber long rifle bullets?"

Hammer threw up his hands in surprise. "Two boxes! *Two* boxes of bullets were in my place!" he said heatedly. "Yeah, they were sitting together on the shelf. I'll bet some *cop* took one box for his own personal use."

More laughter spilled from the jurors. With his unbridled honesty, Hammer unintentionally turned the tables on the defense. In a situation when many would try to sugar-coat their actions, Hammer instead won over the jurors with straightforwardness. For the rest of the trial, his testimony was largely accepted as truthful and believable. He told about Anderson repeatedly discussing using a gun rather than a knife to frighten a victim. There were the countless conversations about the best way to dispose of a victim, such as "dismembering and scattering parts of the body" and "burying, burning, or throwing out other evidence along the road." Another idea was to cut the hands, feet, and head off of a body so it couldn't be identified through fingerprints or dental records. When Hammer finally left the stand, the prosecution's case had solidified.

Glen Walker
Mid-April 1997

THEN GLEN WALKER appeared in the picture. During the Streyle investigation, one of Anderson's coworkers brought an answering machine tape into the Sioux Falls Police Department. Glen Walker had called this coworker and left a message saying that someone should mention that Robert was out looking for a country church that his wife, Elaine, and mother wanted to locate and attend. The tape had Walker saying, "This will help take away some of the premeditation."

It was obvious to the coworker that Walker was trying to create an alibi for Anderson being near the Streyle home, by suggesting that while looking for this church, Anderson just happened to come across the Bible Camp at the Streyles'. The obvious conclusion was that Walker wouldn't leave a message of this nature unless he owed Anderson something. The detectives knew that Walker was somehow involved but didn't know anything beyond that. To put anxiety and pressure on Walker, the prosecution subpoenaed him, which meant he had to come to the trial and, as far as Walker knew, he may have to get up and testify. But the prosecution had no intention of calling him to the stand. It was a strategy to make him nervous and it worked. Throughout the proceedings, Walker became increasingly edgy regarding his past deeds and hatched a plan to sidestep any potential charges he might face for his association with Anderson. Walker got himself a lawyer.

During the trial, Walker's lawyer approached Attorney General Barnett.

"Glen Walker can tell you where Larisa Dumansky is buried in exchange for immunity," the attorney said.

The trial was reaching its peak, and everyone on the legal team was swamped with work, but obviously this was critical. Barnett directed Walker to talk to Minnehaha County prosecutor Dave Nelson. Walker's attorney made the same offer to Nelson.

"What do you need immunity from?" Nelson asked Walker.

"One time when me and Rob were out driving, he showed me the grove of trees where he buried Larisa. I can show you where it is."

Nelson was ready with an immediate response. "You didn't do anything illegal then. You don't need immunity. It's not against the law on your part if someone shows you where a body is buried. We would like to know where Larisa's body is, though, if you would be willing to tell us."

Walker's willingness to turn against his friend was astonishing to those who knew them. Friends with Anderson since elementary school, Walker was diagnosed with dyslexia, and his reading problems made him the target of school bullies. Anderson always came to his defense. Walker said, "We always joked that he did the thinking, and I did the heavy lifting." It was a statement that had come eerily true. Those who profile serial killers frequently note that sociopaths have an ability to exploit weaknesses in others in order to manipulate people to do things they normally wouldn't do. Though he appeared to be protecting Walker, it was more likely that the cold-blooded killer was merely taking advantage of an underdog.

Walker discussed the options with his attorney. To the satisfaction of the prosecution team, Walker decided to show the location of the gravesite. Walker would appear a hero while also exonerating himself from the crimes. At the time it seemed like a foolproof plan for him, but it soon blew up in his face.

There was no time for the prosecution to focus on Walker's information during an intense kidnapping trial. The information was turned over to the Minnehaha County State's Attorney, who pursued this lead while the trial continued. After weeks of testimony, the trial came to a head. Barnett gave the closing statements by saying that the evidence was overwhelming in pointing to Anderson's guilt.

"He has duct tape and receipts and paint and handcuffs and bullet casings and blood and fibers and hair all hanging off him. He's covered with evidence. It's taped on." To emphasize his point, Barnett walked to the evidence table and slowly held up several pieces of evidence one by one for the jury to view a final time.

As the prosecution team wrapped up with emotionally impacting comments, two jurors broke down sobbing. The whole experience took its toll on everyone involved. In a rare and shocking move, Anderson's counsel waived his right to closing statements.

The jury of ten women and two men deliberated for five hours and during this time took three separate votes. Each time it was a unanimous guilty decision. The jurors felt he was responsible due to the state's convincing evidence. However, they took several hours to continue discussing the case to give Anderson as fair a shake as possible. Several weeks later at his sentencing on July 18, 1997, one year after Piper went missing, Judge McMurchie imposed the maximum: life in prison. Anderson could make a statement and began by complaining that he didn't get a fair trial and claiming that he now accepted Jesus Christ. Yet moments later he turned with scornful eyes to the prosecuting attorneys at a nearby table and said, "I hope you rot in hell!"

Members of Piper's family addressed Anderson, asking him to reveal the location of Piper's body and encouraging him to seek God while in prison. Anderson, however, remained stone-faced. Later, outside the courthouse and amid a flurry of questions from half a dozen journalists, one inquiry stood out.

"What are your feelings about Anderson's final comment directed at you?"

"I may rot in hell, but it sure won't be for sending him to prison," Barnett answered to the satisfaction of many standing around him.

Afterward, Anderson continued to profess his innocence.

"Why would I do something like this? I am married, very happily, to a very loving wife, very good-looking and attractive wife," Anderson said. He also blamed his attorneys for not bringing up what he considered inconsistencies at trial. "I'm not very happy with my attorneys. I expected more from them." Anderson's arrogance reached a peak when he demanded that police find Piper's body, which he presumed would prove his innocence. As though he were in charge of the case, Anderson added that he didn't want to hear any excuses from investigators. He demanded that they do their job and find her body. Throughout interviews and contact with Anderson, it became increasingly clear that he operated from the mindset of a typical sociopath who projected his own faults onto others. He accused the prosecution team of trying to hide the truth and refusing to look at the evidence. His wife, Elaine, questioned how the state could be so sure that Piper was dead. People close to Anderson claimed he was good to his family and could have never committed this crime. Barnett had a comeback for this weak defense. "Anderson is like many predators, including a bear. They'll protect their own cubs while viciously killing others."

Newspapers in the area published the cost of Anderson's trial, which was one of the most expensive cases the state had seen. Citizens were appalled with all that he was provided: the best lawyers, private investigators, experts in a variety of fields, and whatever else his attorneys felt necessary. It was the equivalent of a judicial spending spree. On the other hand, middle-class citizens accused of crimes cannot afford to hire the best lawyers, and many do not qualify for a court-appointed attorney.

Anderson then began making a slew of complaints, aiming some at the jury by saying he felt there were too many females. "…anytime you discuss rape in front of a jury that's a majority of women, women are…offended by the remarks and they tend to believe things more," he said. Anderson continued to claim he did not own a 9mm handgun.

Barnett responded to the complaints by saying that Anderson had a chance to give his side and now he could tell his sob story to the warden.

People affected by the crimes needed to move forward as best they could. Piper's parents were in the midst of dealing with two of life's emotional extremes. As soon as the heartrending trial ended, they had to pick up and head back to Texas. Their son was graduating that day from college and would be getting married the following week. As for the prosecutors, they had little time to celebrate or move on from Anderson's crimes. Some very unexpected and serious information was brought to the attention of the attorney general. It was the evidence they needed for a death sentence.

Finding Larisa's Remains

A SQUAD CAR bounced down the rutted, narrow dirt road near Lake Vermillion. Walker was in tow to point out the spot where Larisa was buried. A team of volunteer law enforcement agents descended on the site to exhume the remains. A tinge of hope permeated the somber atmosphere. A northwest wind flowed across the open fields and through the valley, swaying the heavy branches of the chokecherry bush beacon-like. It wasn't possible to dig around the tangle of brush, so they hacked back the branches to gain access to the soil. The volunteers labored beneath the open sky long after their shirts became saturated with perspiration. They proceeded with the delicate operation of gently removing dirt one shallow layer at a time in a horizontal pattern. The soil was placed in a sift box and shaken side to side to separate the loose dirt from solid objects atop the screened box. The searchers used the same methods archaeologists practice in finely brushing and logging unearthed items. The steady click of a camera recorded the step-by-step process. They searched the area around the gravesite using a small backhoe which turned up pieces that were somehow scattered up to 200 yards from the gravesite.

In the end, the volunteers found a rib, fragments of a pair of blue jeans including its leather patch, duct tape, bones from an ankle and wrist with duct tape attached, fifteen 9mm shell casings around the gravesite, six 9mm slugs within the gravesite, two jersey gloves bleached by the sun, a white athletic sock with two foot bones inside, and two women's Dexter leather sandals—one with a toe bone inside. It was far less than what they anticipated, and this led to many discussions about what happened to the rest of the remains. One theory was that animals scattered the bones from the shallow grave. The remains were sent to a lab for DNA analysis to ascertain whether they belonged to Larisa. Then began the wait for the results to be returned from the lab.

The Con Cons the Con
Late Summer, 1997

ON THE CREST of a rolling hill in the northern part of Sioux Falls sits the expansive state penitentiary compound. First constructed from timber as a territorial prison in 1881, the facility went through many renovations. Now old block walls resembling a medieval castle butt up to modern brick buildings to create a varied appearance. Capital punishment in the state of South Dakota also went through changes. Inmates at the turn of the century met their fate with the hangman's noose, but by the 1940s it was the electric chair. In 1947, "Old Sparky" would be used for the first and only time on George Sitts, who murdered a man during a botched robbery and escaped from a Minnesota jail, fleeing to South Dakota. Near the town of Spearfish, he shot and killed special agent Tom Matthews and Butte County Sheriff Dave Malcom, and for these two murders, Sitts was sentenced to death. On April 8, 1947, while strapped into the electric chair, 33-year-old Sitts's last words were, "This is the first time authorities helped me *escape* prison." The executioner then threw the switch four times, and Sitts was pronounced dead. Today in the death row area of the prison sits the lethal injection gurney with leather straps to hold the condemned inmate in place for the insertion of the needle that carries deadly compounds. Within the maximum-security prison in Sioux Falls, there is a pod deemed the notorious "ad seg" area, where the iron-toned clatter of incarceration echoes down the tiers. It is considered a prison within a prison and used to isolate inmates who are chronic discipline problems, a risk to prison operations, or sentenced to death and awaiting lethal injection. Ad seg is the worst for the worst.

Residing alone in ad seg was Jeremy Brunner, quick-witted and well-schooled in the skills required for penitentiary survival; he was a savvy convict. With an obesely bulging stomach and burly face, it often surprised people when they discovered he was only in his early twenties. Brunner cut his teeth in the Michigan penal system where a string of convictions resulted in several lock-ups beginning in his early teenage years. He eventually made his way to South Dakota, and keeping with his past history, he proceeded to get charged with several crimes that landed him in the state penitentiary with a five-year sentence for robbery. Prior to his trial, however, he spent time in the Minnehaha County Jail, where he caused so many disruptions that the warden of the penitentiary immediately placed Brunner in ad seg upon his arrival.

Brunner wasn't one to let his guard down. Growing up fending for himself resulted in a natural knack for grabbing opportunity wherever and however he could. He was a con's con. His knowledge of the criminal code rivaled that of seasoned lifers. In spite of this, he arrived at ad seg on edge due to a situation that could cause his entire prison sentence to be wrought with difficulty. The problem was that his past criminal history consisted of what inmates would consider mediocre crimes that would give him little status among the prison population. He'd be at the bottom of the pecking order, and that would cloud every minute of every day that he spent behind bars. Brunner wasn't one to sit back and hope for the best. He manipulated his world to get what he needed; what he needed was an impressive criminal history to boost his image and give him "street status." Telling exaggerated stories about their criminal history is common among inmates, but the officials in the prison had yet to run across anyone who pulled off the ruse that Brunner concocted.

Brunner sought out a criminal associate with access to a prison computer. He had the guy create an official-looking rap sheet that falsified Brunner's charges in order to inflate his criminal status. The list included him beating a murder charge in Oklahoma. Brunner carried the rap sheet around so others could view it until word of his "accomplishment" was thoroughly solidified among the inmates. So skilled in the art of coming out on top, he managed to obtain the valuable document in exchange for two cans of chewing tobacco.

(The following page shows the fake rap sheet Brunner had an accomplice develop for him.)

Department of Corrections
South Dakota State Penitentiary
Central Files

****

INMATE ID: 32614   NAME: Brunner, Jeremy D.

SOURCE: Department of Public Safety, Wayne County, Detroit, MI

Alias(es): "Kilo"

Address(es): 1312 Imperial Ave., Detroit, MI 48185

Gang Affiliation: Yes

Name/Title: Hoover Crips

Disposition: 1) Abusive - Firm Gang Association/Ties
              2) Known Firearm Carrier/Extremely Dangerous

Primary Criminal Activity: Narcotic Sales - Gang Related

Contacts/Associations: See Wayne County Gang Identification
                           Unit Files: "Hoover Crips"

Criminal History

        Wayne Metro: 1990 - Felony Drive-by Shooting **Reduced
                            to Unlawful Use (Discharge) Firearm
                            in Residential Area

        Wayne Metro: 1993 - Assault w/Intent of Great Bodily Harm
                            -less/Attempted Murder/Manslaughter

        Wayne Metro: 1993 - Possession of a Controlled Substance
                            -Cocaine/more than 60 gr.

                    Bond Posted - All Counts (cash)

        FBI: Tulsa, Oklahoma
              First Degree Murder **Dismissed**
              Possession of Stolen Vehicle **Convicted**

Previous Incarceration - Penitentiary: Wayne Correctional

Time Served/Penitentiary: 2 yrs.

                End Query Information "Criminal History"
** **

1997 found Robert Leroy Anderson also locked in the ad seg wing of the same penitentiary. Depending on their sentence, inmates could request a cellmate, which was often preferable to being totally isolated. Having heard of Brunner's reputation, Anderson put in a request to become cellmates with Brunner. It was approved by the administration and Brunner accepted. Anderson eagerly packed his few possessions for the cell change.

Over the hollow sounds of closing cell doors and the occasional angry shout from an inmate, the two had nothing to do but talk. The seemingly endless hours behind bars, with only a one-hour exercise break per day, led to intriguing conversations between Brunner and Anderson as both tended to be long-winded. Anderson was anxious to know how Brunner beat the murder conviction in Oklahoma but wasn't savvy enough to know how to play his cards. His question came off as desperate, which Brunner picked up immediately.

"I pinned the homicide on someone else by planting evidence at his house and paying a witness to falsely testify against him. It worked." Brunner paused to gauge Anderson's reaction and deduced that he had his cellmate right where he wanted him. "The feds dropped the charges on me, and that fool got hit with the murder rap." Brunner added intricate details to this story he was confidently spinning as he went along.

Anderson paused for several minutes before cautiously asking, "Do you think you could help me pin my charge on someone else?"

The ever-watchful Brunner sensed a rare opportunity, one that came along perhaps once in a lifetime to only the most fortunate of inmates. He'd landed amid a grossly unequal fight in which he was the heavyweight who would toy with his slight and disadvantaged opponent before going for the knockout. It was second nature for Brunner to appear somewhat disinterested. "Let me think about this, and we'll talk again. I'll make inquiries when my brother visits."

When the topic was brought up again, an anxious Anderson sat on the edge of his bed, hands folded in his lap, and listened intently.

"Okay. First, I need to know everything that the cops know, everything they don't know, and everything only the killer would know about the murder." He paused to let the gravity of the situation set in. "And since everyone knows you killed the Streyle woman, is there anyone else you've bumped off, and is there anyone else who might know it so we can take care of them, too? If I don't have all the facts, and I mean *all* the facts, our plan will fall apart."

In a detached way, as if he were reliving the crimes, Anderson shared his most guarded secrets. His eyes, that moments prior were normal, now had a faraway look of rapture. He began confessing intimate details about the murder of Piper and Larisa while Brunner took impeccable mental notes and maintained a poker face despite the overwhelming joy he felt inside at the fortunate opportunity into which he stumbled. Once Anderson started talking, he couldn't stop. He exploded piñata-like with information, and the two talked until 4:00 AM. The same thing happened the following night and then the night after that. Brunner later explained that he couldn't get Anderson to shut up once he started spilling information.

"Give me some more time. Let me discuss this with my people out on the streets, and then we'll talk some more," Brunner said with finality.

Brunner had a talent akin to that of an FBI profiler. It was a rare gift. It didn't take him long to observe a person's body language and voice in order to make judgments about the person's character and personality. He was rarely wrong. He strung Anderson along and allowed trust to build in order to squeeze every bit of information he could from his surprisingly gullible cellmate, knowing that even an amateur like Anderson wouldn't spill all his secrets at once. So Brunner baited Anderson with some crushing news. His street connections were concerned that any lapses in information would cause the whole scheme to backfire. They weren't convinced and wanted more details.

"If you've held anything back, we need to know it now."

Anderson told about the tire poppers and how they failed to get him a girl. He blamed Walker for the botched attempt to kidnap Amy Anderson on the highway, saying, "The coward froze up." He told about the washable paint to disguise his Bronco, and about kidnapping, raping, and killing Larisa Dumansky. Then he admitted with pride why he had the long wooden dowels in his toolbox. He used them to penetrate and sexually abuse women.

The stone-faced Brunner took it all in.

Anderson clenched his jaw and asked curtly, "Whatcha gonna do about that gutless Glen Walker? He's living in Kansas City and knows where Larisa's buried. He has to go."

"Okay. I know a guy with no alibi. We can pin all these crimes on him. I have a girl who'll date this guy, and at the right time she'll plant evidence in his house or car. Then she'll call the police and report that this guy tried to rape her. If we do it right, your lawyer should get you a mistrial that will set you free."

Anderson raised his fists above his head in a silent cheer.

"As far as Walker is concerned, my brother will find out where his parents live in Kansas City, stake it out, and eliminate him," he said to Anderson, who nodded in agreement. "I need to get items to plant that will frame this guy. What do you have, and how can my outside people get the items?"

Anderson hesitated. He didn't want to give up the souvenir jewelry he took off Larisa and Piper. These trophies were his most prized possessions, as the items allowed him to relive the thrill of the hunt and kill. Just holding the women's jewelry gave him a stimulating surge. But his desire to get out of prison was more powerful than the intense longing to keep the prized souvenirs. Reluctantly he disclosed that he took a necklace with a heart-shaped pendant from Larisa and a Black Hills gold wedding band from Piper. He also had two sets of handcuffs and his 9mm pistol. All the items were stashed in the ceiling rafters at his mom's house. They were in the basement above the door jamb of his childhood bedroom.

"Okay. We can pull this off in steps, and it's going to cost you in steps. I can get the wheels turning on this for $2,000. You have to make arrangements for $500 to be put into my brother's bank account for a down payment. The balance of the $2,000 will be due once you get released," Brunner explained. Then, leaving nothing to chance, he had Anderson sketch two maps. One was the floor layout of Anderson's mom's house pointing out where to find the items to be planted. The second map was the location of where Walker lived in Kansas City so the hit man could find him and also steal Walker's car. Brunner suggested that they fence Walker's stolen car so Anderson could get some of his cash back for this deal.

"Is there any, and I mean any other information that nobody but you would know about that I might be able to use to set up this guy?" Brunner said, pressing for what he was sure was more information. Anderson's response was the big ace that the shrewd Brunner was waiting for. Now he was ready to make the move to guarantee not Anderson's freedom but his own.

Jeremy Brunner Plays His Hand

IT WAS SECOND nature for Brunner to play by the convict's code, a way to minimize problems behind bars. Prison was like that. There are unwritten taboos that can earn an inmate a slit throat. At the top of that list is being a snitch, and "flapping to the man" was something Brunner had never done despite having had numerous opportunities to do so. Over the course of several days, however, Anderson shared increasingly detailed information about the rapes and murders he committed to the point that the man seemed unable to stop talking about them. The violent nature of the crimes combined with the fact that four children lost a mother was too much for even Brunner to stomach. Anderson's perversions removed him from the protective umbrella of the convict code and placed him in the same arena generally reserved for prison outcasts such as pedophiles. Anderson was fair game.

Brunner spoke to his mother about the conversations with Anderson, and she agreed that the information should be shared with authorities. In fact, son and mother decided she would be the one to contact the prison administration and drop just enough information to spark their interest in talking to Brunner. Nearly every day in prison, an inmate requests to speak to prison staff regarding giving information in exchange for a reduced sentence, so it was likely that the guards would refuse or ignore Brunner's request. A common saying is that a jailhouse snitch's information isn't worth a bucket of warm spit. It's one convict's word against another's. Such testimony is quickly discredited by the defense attorney because the information given by the informant is self-serving. *This witness has a shady background, and he is not a Good Samaritan offering this testimony for the good of justice. This is a jailhouse snitch who fabricated a story to buy his freedom.* A wary jury often sides with the defense regarding these questionable witnesses, but Brunner was not typical.

Based on the call by Brunner's mother, prison caseworker Darin Young met with Brunner and listened to what he had to say about Anderson's crimes.

"I only want to speak with Mark Barnett about the important things I know," Brunner said.

"Look, Mr. Barnett is the state's attorney general. He's not going to just hop down here and talk to you based on your word. You have to give me something," Young explained.

Brunner sat in deep thought; he had an enviable knack for being able to quickly size up a situation and turn it in his favor. He played an ace right from the start. "You people think Anderson took that kid's tent to put Piper's body in, but you've got it wrong. There was a struggle in the house, and Anderson's pistol went off. It shot a hole through the tent and into the floor. If you go back to that bedroom, you'll find a bullet hole in the floor under the carpet. He took the tent because it had a bullet hole through it and a gunpowder burn. Check it out. Then come back and see me."

A less experienced con might have given away all he knew at once in hopes of persuading officials to listen, but Brunner held his hand. It was all he needed to say. Young called a DCI agent, who in turn called Vance. He happened to be home, and went into the bedroom and pulled back the carpet in Nathan's bedroom. There indeed was a bullet hole in the floor. Severson and other investigators were sent out. When they found the bullet hole in the floor, they inserted a metal rod into the hole of the bedroom floor. The rod gave the exact angle the bullet traveled. They crawled under the trailer house and used the steel rod as their guide to determine where to search for the slug. Using only their bare hands, they scraped away at the dirt and quickly found the 9mm slug.

This made sense when combined with information Shaina provided about the mean man coming back to the trailer and taking the tent. Unsupervised, she and Nathan wandered out into the yard, and Anderson made them go back in. It was later determined that he not only took the tent but also his wristwatch, which broke during the struggle with Piper.

When word of the bullet hole reached the attorney general's office in Pierre, South Dakota, Long and Barnett, along with Patty Froning, were on a plane within thirty minutes headed to Sioux Falls to meet with Brunner. Brunner sauntered in, and as he sat down, the chair creaked beneath his immense body. In this small interview room, Barnett sat across from him while Long was behind a one-way mirror observing and typing up an affidavit to get the anticipated search warrants. Barnett launched the videotaped interview by discussing a deal with Brunner.

"You provided us with the bullet hole in the bedroom, and as you've claimed, if you can produce the jewelry, gun, and handcuffs related to these murders as well as other details, that would be huge in solving the crimes. I can't guarantee I can get you a pardon. I need to speak with the people who have the power to make this decision, but I promise I'll do all I can for you."

Brunner stretched, yawned, and folded his arms across his chest. "I understand."

"So, Anderson opened up to you about these murders."

"He wanted me to help him get out of prison. I told Anderson we can plant evidence on a dude I know who has no alibi, and that dude will look guilty, and then a good lawyer should be able to get an acquittal for him. But I told Anderson I have to know everything the cops know, and especially things they don't know in order to pin the murders on this ghost dude. I'll call him Mr. Ghost. I didn't push too hard for info because I wanted Anderson to open up so he wouldn't get suspicious. Now he trusts me and tells me everything. I told Anderson we needed evidence to plant in Mr. Ghost's car then place a 911 call and the cops will find the stuff connected to the murder in Mr. Ghost's car. So, Anderson tells me where in his mom's house he hid the pistol, handcuffs, and jewelry he took for souvenirs off the two women."

Brunner went on to explain how Anderson drew a map of his mom's house so that the items could be retrieved by Brunner's people on the street, and a map was drawn to where Walker lived in Kansas City. He also explained how the women were killed and what had been done to them sexually before they died.

"Once Anderson opened up and told me about the murders and rapes, he couldn't stop talking. He relished in reliving it. You could see it in his eyes, and he talked about it over and over."

"Did he talk about any other murders or if he wanted to keep doing these things?" Barnett asked.

"He didn't mention any other murders, but he said he learned a lot from getting caught. Anderson said that if he got out of prison, he would do it some more but would be smarter and not get caught. He can't stop it. In fact, he told me he has been focusing on the prison nurse and that she's pretty and would like to do her. He even smirked and said both those women he raped said that their husbands were the only men they'd ever been with. Anderson told me that if we both get out of prison, we could work together to rape women. I was sickened by the things he's telling me, but I got to play it cool and act hard. "

"This is important information," Barnett confirmed.

"I don't like being a snitch, and I've never done it, but this is special. The stuff Rob Anderson was doing was ruining kids' lives, so it's special, and that's why I'm talking, and you people need to know this stuff."

Brunner handed over the hand-drawn map to where the hidden items could be found. It was a huge break in the case. With a signed search warrant and the map, a team of investigators headed to the house of Anderson's mother to look for the physical evidence supposedly hidden in a ceiling.

Murderous Mementos

WITH MAP IN hand, drawn by Anderson himself, the police went to Ruth Anderson's house. Following the diagram, it took less than five minutes to find what they were looking for. Using a small, handheld mirror, investigators looked into the basement rafters to locate the evidence. Before removing them, they took photographs to demonstrate how the items had been stashed. Piper's wedding ring and Larisa's necklace had been woven together with the chain of the necklace looped several times through the ring. An investigator removed each piece, allowed it to be photographed, then put it a special evidence bag which was labeled and not allowed to be touched by anyone else to limit the number of people who encountered it. They repeated the same process with the 9mm gun and clip and two pairs of handcuffs. Collectively, it was the mother lode of evidence, and now they had their smoking gun.

Based on information from Brunner, another search was conducted to find Piper's body. They searched along the Big Sioux River, and divers descended into promising areas, but their visibility was limited due to the murky water. Everyone was looking for an area with a log or debris jam, as Anderson described placing her in such a location. An anatomy professor from the University of Sioux Falls joined the search to help distinguish human from animal bones found.

Sustained Strength
August 26, 1997

SOFT-SPOKEN AND optimistic, Bill Dumansky spent the better part of two years searching for Larisa. Living in the Ukraine taught him that life could be both tough and unfair, but he overcame both with hard work and a determined attitude. He kept thinking that she was possibly being kept against her will. Bill's oldest daughter had a nightmare that her mother was being held captive deep in the woods where no one could find her. As horrible as the possibility seemed, it was preferable to Larisa being dead. Bill was adamant that she didn't leave on her own and hoped to someday be reunited with her. He hired psychics and private investigators, whom some people close to the case accused of taking Bill's money and running. Then on August 26th, he received a call to come to the police department to identify some of her belongings. Vance received a similar call, and the two arrived at the police station at about the same time. Long, Barnett, and several investigators also gathered there immediately after finding the stash of jewelry, handcuffs, and the weapon, and their mood was celebratory. They ordered pizza and were pumped about the good fortune of getting tipped off to this physical evidence that would clearly be significant in solidifying murder charges against Anderson.

When the wedding ring and heart-shaped pendant were laid out for Vance and Bill to identify, the atmosphere went somber. Vance, having been through a kidnapping trial, already had time to come to terms that Piper was gone. But for Bill, the sight of Larisa's gold necklace hit him with the realization that his wife was indeed dead. Bill's shoulders slumped, and the life seemed to all but go out of him as well. He was heartbroken, and the room stilled. After an uncomfortable silence, with no one managing to conjure just the right words, Vance quietly stepped over to Bill and put his arm around him. He led Bill to a room where they spent a long time alone. No one but the two men ever knew what words of comfort and eternal hope Vance must have spoken, but when they returned, Bill was composed and ready to move forward. It was a bond that only survivors who had lost their wives in such a tragic way could understand.

"Oh, Boy"

THE PROSECUTING TEAM did not rest easy despite Brunner agreeing to testify. There were too many unknowns they couldn't ignore. Brunner was a known drug dealer. If they let Brunner out of prison before he testified, several bad things could happen. There was a distinct possibility he could get bumped off. At 400 pounds and 5'8", they worried about him having a heart attack or other serious health problems. Even if neither of those things happened, it was highly likely Brunner would disappear into the seedy criminal underworld never to be seen again. There were at least three warrants out for his arrest in Michigan alone. On the other hand, prison is a dangerous place for an informant like Brunner. Because of this, Long made an unusual request to depose Brunner in prison. This meant that Brunner would be interviewed, and his responses written down for later use in court. If Brunner was not deposed and died or did not show up at trial, none of his statements could be used as evidence at trial. It would be the only time in Long's forty-year career he would use this rare legal maneuver. The prosecution requested permission from the court to do this, but the defense tried to block the move in hopes that Brunner would happen to disappear. After some drawn-out arguments, the judge ruled in Long's favor.

It took two days to interview Brunner and preserve his testimony in a manner that would hold up in court. Then true to his word, Barnett began the process of rewarding Brunner for the information he provided in strengthening the case for Larisa's and Piper's rape and murder trials. Barnett brought Brunner in front of the judge who had originally sentenced him to the penitentiary, since this judge still held the power to modify Brunner's sentence.

"We want you to reward him for the information he provided and reduce his sentence to time served and put him on probation," Barnett requested.

The judge agreed, and Brunner was released in mid-November of 1997. Brunner was, unfortunately, the perfect example of the expression *you can't change the spots on a leopard*. He gained the respect of many people for what he was willing to do for justice, and for this he earned his freedom. However, he could never be free from himself. In less than three weeks, Long received a call.

Brunner sold fifty hits of LSD to an undercover narcotics officer. This too was a scam. The drugs were analyzed and determined to be fake, which is still a misdemeanor. This led to a dilemma. Should Brunner be arrested and charged with a probation violation, or should they look the other way since it was only a misdemeanor? The decision was made to issue a warrant for Brunner's arrest and try to revoke his probation. Perhaps the judge would send him back to the penitentiary, where he would at least be alive and available for the upcoming trial. No one could have fathomed the dysfunctional twist Brunner would throw into the plan.

Long dreaded the implications this would have regarding Brunner's testimony. The convict's testimony would already be subject to scrutiny by the defense, and now Brunner had put an even bigger target on his back. *This man couldn't follow the rules of society for the short time he was back on the street, and we're supposed to believe his testimony?* Another hitch was that Brunner could turn uncooperative and refuse to testify further.

Brunner was arrested based on the warrant and transported to the Minnehaha County Jail.

THE INCIDENT WITH the fake LSD could possibly have been smoothed over if Brunner could have managed to be a model citizen while incarcerated. Unfortunately, he blew that chance even before arriving in his cell. He was subjected to a strip search while being booked into the county jail. The hefty Brunner had tucked some small packets of dope into a fat roll on the side of his belly, and these were the real deal. He had half an ounce of methamphetamine, enough to be considered a dealer.

So, Long received yet another call informing him of this new development.

"Oh, boy," was all he could muster.

Because of these sins, the anger of God is coming.

—Colossians 3:6 (NLT)

The Long Hours

COFFEE ... MEETINGS ... DEADLINES ... typing affidavits ... more coffee to help him keep going at a hectic pace. A stale sandwich with a few half-moon bites eaten from it sat next to a pile of papers. Work was the priority. Eating occurred when a spare minute could be found. There had never been a time in Long's career when the stakes were so high, the pressure so intense, and the hours so long. Over 1,000 pieces of evidence were sent to the state crime lab and over 200 of these would be presented at trial in Sioux Falls. It was essential that physical evidence be processed correctly, or the case could be lost on a technicality. A piece of key evidence could be denied at trial if the judge deemed that it was mishandled. For example, Anderson's 9mm pistol. Every person who touched the handgun from the time it was found hidden until it came into the courtroom was accountable for its condition and would be called on the witness stand to confirm his or her role in handling the evidence. It was the job of the defense to object to each piece of evidence, and a good lawyer could argue that the pistol could not be submitted because someone who did not testify touched it. *The handgun could have been altered, and the firing pin marks on the recovered shell casings are now baseless.* A variety of angles could be employed to taint the pistol's impact if the trail of people who handled it was not carefully documented. This was especially vital with the handgun due to Anderson's left thumb print being found on the clip.

Thus, when an investigator found the 9mm in the ceiling at the home of Anderson's mother, he made sure the pistol was not touched by anyone else, immediately sealed in a bag, placed in the trunk of a squad car, and driven directly to the crime lab. This way the investigator and crime lab personnel would be the only ones who needed to be called to testify. And so, this same caution had to be given to every piece of physical evidence that would be brought before the jury. It was a tedious and time-consuming process.

Hammer provided information that the metal poppers were used to flatten the tire of an unsuspecting female. He also said that the devices were painted gray, black, or pinkish-red to match the three road colors found in South Dakota and therefore to camouflage the metal so it was less visible on the road. One day Long was at the state crime lab in Pierre with Anderson's defense team. The physical evidence was laid out for the defense attorneys so they could prepare their arguments for Anderson. Long looked at a tire popper and then happened to glance at the bondage board. At that moment it came to him, and he solved one of the mysteries. He picked up a tire popper, walked it over to the bondage board, and placed it inside the shadowy silhouette. The device fit perfectly, and its color matched. Anderson had spray painted the poppers on the bondage board. Long asked the lab personnel to compare the paint on the poppers to the paint on the bondage board. They matched. Agents returned to Anderson's shed and confiscated a can of spray paint. This same paint was on the board and the poppers.

There was ongoing pressure from the public to not spend taxpayer dollars on a trial for a man already serving a life sentence. However, many people felt that the families of Larisa and Piper deserved to know that the person responsible for their deaths would be punished to the full extent of the law despite the cost. The decision was made to move forward and seek the death penalty to ensure that this killer would not have the chance to commit more crimes. To some it added insult to injury when Anderson demanded an additional lawyer and a private investigator to help with his case.

Long, Froning, and Barnett prepared dozens of subpoenas every day during the trial in order to get all the witnesses into court, and this information was given to Anderson's defense team so they in turn could prepare. The prosecution team also spent late hours preparing witnesses as to what questions might arise on the stand. *Only answer questions directly. Give no more information than what is required. Do not let the defense get you angry or riled up. Always tell the truth.* These were some of their standard tips for being a good witness.

A typical trial day for Long began at 5:00 AM when he would get up and review his notes. At 6:00 AM he'd go on a two-mile run, shower, eat, and get to the courthouse by 8:00 AM. After a day in court, he'd head home at 5:00 PM, take a one-hour nap, eat, and work until midnight.

Long and Froning spent two and a half years working virtually full time on the Anderson trials. They started preparing for the kidnapping trial in July of 1996 and didn't stop until everything was wrapped up after the second trial in April of 1999. The road in between was filled with even more Anderson family dysfunction. Astonishingly, it was only one month after Robert was accused of abducting Piper when Lee Iver was charged with attempted murder for stabbing the two people in their home. Then in December 1997, Anderson's father joined all his sons in prison when he was sentenced to two years after his third offense in five years for operating a vehicle under the influence of alcohol.

In the Name of Justice

THE PROSECUTION STOOD poised with a strong case, its foundation courtesy of Brunner. Despite the stunt of hiding drugs in his fat roll, Brunner would still testify against Anderson. Even though there were inmates who branded Brunner a snitch, he stayed strong in his belief that Anderson's crimes didn't deserve to fall within the convict code of honor. But the pressure on him mounted. There were endless death threats from other inmates, so much so that he received counseling to help him deal with the stress. Brunner only had eighteen months left of his sentence, which is a short time for someone with his background. He paid a price for stepping forward. Some inmates supported him, but others threw urine at his cell and yelled obscenities and threats. His determination did not waver, which lent credence to his statement that testifying against Anderson was the right thing to do. Brunner was transported directly from the prison to the courthouse. So vital was this testimony that even decades later, the prosecutors felt deep gratitude toward Brunner for his part in bringing Anderson to justice.

Long wanted the murder trials of Larisa and Piper to be combined, since the logical conclusion of all the evidence was that the homicides were entwined. The defense requested that the crimes be tried separately. It was a move that held the possibility of getting an acquittal on one or the other in separate trials. It was not a request made lightly. The prosecution put in enormous hours assembling a two-inch binder summarizing each piece of evidence and the expected statements of all sixty witnesses they were prepared to call. The prosecution brought in the highly respected and experienced FBI sex crimes profiler, Roy Hazelwood, who compared the Dumansky and Streyle evidence. It was his professional conclusion that the specifics of the two crimes pointed to the same perpetrator being responsible for both abductions and murders. It was logical that Anderson's sexual habits followed a pattern. Three of his former girlfriends had been interviewed, and they revealed that when it came to having sex, Anderson was aggressive and would not take no for an answer. Hazelwood's findings had a significant impact on the judge's decision, which was to side with the prosecution. Anderson would face charges for the rapes and murders of Larisa and Piper at one trial.

Next, it was announced that the death penalty would be sought, a statement that was splashed across newspaper headlines the following day. Well before the pool of jurors showed up, both sides did background checks on each potential juror, an arduous process. And then came the lengthy process of questioning potential jurors. Each one would be interviewed independently. It takes a specific type of person who can vote to put another human being to death. An individual who could never vote for the death penalty and anyone who was overly in favor of capital punishment would be eliminated right away by either the prosecution or defense attorneys. The goal for Long was to pick jurors who, under the right circumstances, would cast a vote for the death penalty.

"I see on your juror questionnaire form that you are Catholic." Long looked up at the middle-aged man and then continued. "The Catholic Church takes a stand against capital punishment. Will this philosophy govern your decision-making, or can you conceive of circumstances where you could sentence a person to death?"

The man sat deep in thought and then answered with a nod, "Yes. There are certain circumstances where I would honestly consider imposing the death penalty."

Long pressed on. "Give me some examples where you feel capital punishment would be justified."

"If the murder was premeditated or if torture was inflicted on the victim, I could vote for a death sentence," the man replied.

Long jotted some notations on the form. This man would be considered as a juror. The questioning went on like this day after day.

Another major problem occurred during jury selection due to Anderson being present throughout this process. It was his legal right to be there, but he couldn't control his impulses around females. He gawked at them, and his eyes moved up and down their bodies with obvious lust. He even leaned forward to get a closer look. It was unnerving to the potential female jurors, so much so that six refused to return to the courtroom a second time with Anderson sitting there.

It took six weeks to settle on enough jurors to hear the case against Anderson. After the drawn-out jury selection process, prosecutors were optimistic about their choices, which included twelve jurors and four alternates. The eight women and eight men who would hear the case could support a death sentence if that time should come.

Long's successful work throughout a challenging kidnapping trial meant that he would again be part of the prosecuting team, which included Froning and Barnett, in the murder trial as well. Long was originally assigned to assist McCook County prosecutor Roger Gerlach with Piper's trial, since she was kidnapped from her home in that county. With the discovery of Larisa's body in that same county, the assumption was made that this was where she took her last breath. Therefore, Long was the logical choice as one of the prosecutors.

Anderson was again surrounded with some of the best lawyers in the state, Dave Palmer, John Schlimgen, and Mike Butler, who were respected, experienced, and competent. Most citizens could only dream of retaining such high-priced attorneys for their own legal needs.

The trial was held in Minnehaha County in Sioux Falls. It was a modern courtroom constructed with varying shades of brown wood paneling, chairs, and tables. The overhead lighting cast a slight yellowish glow to the wood. To the side of the elevated judge's seat, an American flag's red, white, and blue seemed excessively bright against the dim setting. The spectators' area was filled, and when Anderson was escorted in through a side door, murmurs spread across the courtroom.

Judge Tim Dallas Tucker presided. Both sides gave their opening statements. The trial proceeded through a variety of phases until finally one of the big stars would shine. Key witness Brunner ambled up to the front and was sworn in. He quickly captivated the courtroom; he was sharp, articulate, and confident. With an occasional glib or witty answer, the spectators were soon hanging on his every word. He explained how he was able to gain Anderson's confidence and lure him into giving information about Larisa's murder and the failed attempt to abduct Amy on the highway near Tea, South Dakota. Brunner explained that Anderson considered himself a serial killer because a serial killer keeps something from each of his victims. Anderson also said that it was exciting to do it, and it's exciting to make a total stranger do whatever you want them to do. Anderson tried his go-to intimidation tactic of fixing a hard stare at Brunner, but to no avail. One of Brunner's specialties was intimidation. He glared right back at the pathetic killer and then calmly proceeded with his testimony.

Emotions ran high when Brunner told about Piper's demise. With a steady demeanor, he explained that after Anderson drove away with Piper, he went to a secluded area by the river that he'd chosen ahead of time. Piper was handcuffed to the bondage board, and he cut her night shirt and underwear off. She was repeatedly raped, and when Anderson was done, he straddled her body and wrapped his hands tightly around her throat. As Piper was being strangled, Anderson positioned himself to look right into her eyes. He was disappointed when she didn't struggle but died passively. He then threw Piper's body onto the front floorboard of his Bronco and placed a blanket over her. Then he boldly drove right through Sioux Falls with the body while en route to some private property where he previously had permission to go fishing along the Big Sioux River. He chose this spot because he wanted a place where there was no current to wash the body downstream. He carried her to a backwash cove where a log and debris jam had developed over the years. He waded into the river carrying her body and pushed it under some dead branches where the current would not be able to move her. This contrasted with what he told a previous cellmate from jail, who reported that Anderson said, "She's down so deep, they'll never find her."

Other evidence to corroborate Brunner's testimony was presented. Prior to the trial, officials recorded a telephone conversation Anderson made from prison to his mother in which he requested that a family member transfer $500 to Brunner's brother in Michigan. This was the exact amount Brunner requested as a down payment for the false plan to bump off Glen Walker.

Though the defense team attacked Brunner's character and motivations to be a state's witness from the start, Brunner demonstrated his true character when he was finished testifying. Although he had nothing to gain, he met with John Potts in an act of compassion. Since Potts was banned from the trial due to threats against Anderson, Brunner shared what he said on the stand. He also answered any questions Potts had regarding what Anderson told Brunner in prison.

Prosecutors wasted no time in clobbering away at Anderson's claim that he was only at the Streyle residence to inquire about the Bible Camp. They used many of the same convincing facts that were used in the kidnapping trial. The painted Bronco, the sales receipts, the black snake root, Piper's torn nightshirt and the piece of it found on the bondage board, a folding knife, and spent shell casings from the shooting range, the Streyle house, and Larisa's grave all with firing pin marks that matched Anderson's 9mm pistol. Then came convincing DNA evidence. Evoking emotion from jurors and spectators alike were the bloodstained blue jeans from Anderson's dirty laundry. With Piper menstruating, her blood was in his blue jeans. The defense brought in forensic experts to question the strength of the DNA exhibits.

DCI agent Jim Severson was attending the trials and one morning walked past the private room used by Anderson and his defense attorneys. Angry shouts spilled into the hallway, so Severson paused to listen. It was Anderson screaming at his lawyers and telling them they were doing a bad job representing him. Severson shook his head at this killer who had the best legal team available yet was so arrogant he was telling them how to do their job.

As the trial proceeded, the prosecutors explained how Larisa was stalked, abducted, and raped. To prove that the remains found by Lake Vermillion belonged to Larisa, the lab needed DNA samples from her parents. The problem was that they lived in Russia. Bill stepped in with a solution. Prior to the trial, he returned to Russia and obtained the necessary blood samples from Larisa's mother and father. Bill was taught how to draw the blood samples, which he did. The DNA results came back and left no doubt that the fragments were indeed Larisa's.

The courtroom tensed with curiosity when testimony was presented about Larisa's gravesite. It was revealed that Anderson frequently discussed differences in the way a body decomposed above ground as opposed to below and the repercussions this could have to someone trying to hide a corpse. He even delved into such details as the benefits of burying a body near a tree to conceal a grave. Before Piper's disappearance, Anderson focused on methods to temporarily change the color of a vehicle to make it harder to connect that vehicle to a crime. Although the jury never heard it, people who followed the case learned through the grapevine that when Anderson murdered Larisa, he also killed her unborn child. Because of the third life that was taken and the sadistic, sexual overtones of his crimes, people in the community began referring to Anderson as a serial killer.

Jamie Hammer again testified against his longtime friend and retold much of the same information he shared during the kidnapping trial. Hammer added that he had purchased Anderson's maroon Monte Carlo. One day Hammer was sitting in the open trunk of the Monte Carlo hooking up stereo speakers when Anderson stopped by. Anderson smugly mentioned, "You're sitting right where I hauled Larisa Dumansky's body around."

The media rolled out daily stories with headlines reading "Prosecutors Pile Up Evidence Before Jury" and "Prosecution's Case Enters 3rd Week." Hearts sunk and tears fell when Vance and Bill gave their life-shattering statements. Dry eyes turned wet upon hearing Vance recall his last words to Piper. "I kissed my wife goodbye and told her that I loved her."

Multitudes of people followed the case closely. They were curious about Bill Dumansky and Vance Streyle. Who were these men who lost their wives in such tragic ways, and would they see justice served in this courtroom? Bill was a caring, devout Christian, and the loss of a wife whom he loved so deeply created a swell of anger toward Anderson. During one pretrial proceeding, Bill referred to Anderson as a "monster," and the defense immediately filed a motion that required their client to be called "the defendant" or "Mr. Anderson" for the remainder of the trial so that the jury did not hear the term "monster." When it came time for Bill to testify, he had to contain his emotions and use the term "the defendant." However, when everyone heard Bill's heartbreaking story, the trial moved another step in favor of the prosecution.

Vance, who was tall, thin, and considered to be sharp-looking, remained poised when he told about Anderson coming to their home on the last day of Bible Camp. Sobbing could be heard when he told the tragic story of losing Piper, and the tear-filled questions from his children about a mean man taking mommy. The tide moved with the force of the prosecution's nearly airtight case against Anderson. Throughout the trial, they selected various brown paper sacks and plastic bags from two large evidence tables to support their allegations against Anderson. There were the walkie-talkies, a collapsible shovel, four condoms, nylon rope, receipts, and a jar of Vaseline among other proof. After four weeks of testimony, both sides gave their final arguments to the jury. Following Judge Tucker's instructions, the jurors filed out of the courtroom to begin the first of what would hopefully be two deliberations. To start, they would determine whether he was guilty. If the verdict was guilty, then the jury would hear more evidence to help them determine the penalty, which could mean life in prison or death. Waves of worry washed over everyone with a stake in the outcome. Long was confident that the jury found Hammer and Brunner credible. The jury was stretched emotionally thin after a long trial, and it was 5:00 PM. One member of the prosecution had to stick close to the courthouse in case the jury asked a question. If so, the judge would compose an answer and then ask the prosecution and defense to make suggestions. Long was chosen for this duty. The hours ticked on, but Long felt confident. The more serious the case, the more likely the jury will take time to reach a verdict. When the clock hit 10:00 PM, the jury retired for the night.

The next morning, the jury reconvened, and Long struggled to maintain a sense of calm. He set silent criteria based on the clock. If the jury went beyond noon, he would become concerned. He fought his mind against playing the "what if" game. What if one of the jurors was holding out and preventing the group from reaching a decision? After two hours, however, they were called back into the courtroom. The jury had reached a decision. Anderson was guilty of murdering Larisa and Piper. Long was satisfied that justice was served after spending two and a half years of his life trying to get the conviction this killer deserved.

Next, the jury deliberated Anderson's penalty. The prosecution silently pondered the outcome; anything less than the death penalty would be a loss. It was a commonly held belief in the legal community that a jury in this county would never return a death penalty. Long's main concern was whether they'd chosen twelve jurors who would impose death for this sadistic killer. There was no reliable way to pick a jury, and they'd relied on a combination of gut instinct and well-worded questions to cull the best they could. To find twelve people who not only agreed with each other but also agreed to put another human to death is a challenge to any prosecutor. Only a jury could decide this with a vote that was unanimous.

THE AMERICAN COURT system is considered to be among the best in the world. Within the system, there are laws and regulations regarding what can or cannot be used as evidence against a defendant in a criminal case in order to give that person the best fighting chance during trial. However, with civil court cases or even a different phase in a criminal trial, the rules change. There is a saying that 100 guilty people should go free before one innocent person is convicted. The O.J. Simpson court cases are examples of how the rules can change. O.J. was found not guilty of murder in the criminal trial, but he lost in the civil suit because rules vary for these separate types of trials.

During Anderson's murder trial, the prosecutors were not allowed to present certain evidence; Amy's testimony about her narrow escape on the dark highway and the tire poppers were two of these. Why? The ruling was that they were not directly related to Piper's and Larisa's murders. This came to an end during the penalty phase, and the gloves were off for the prosecutors. Since Anderson had been found guilty of murder, the prosecutors and the defense could present evidence showing his character. The prosecution showed that he had tried to abduct other women and if allowed to live would kill again. He was such an evil person that he indeed deserved death. The jurors then heard Amy tell the terrible story of nearly falling victim to Anderson's plan to kidnap and rape her. The day before the attempted abduction of Amy, he purchased several items to be used in the crime such as starting fluid, which is 50 percent ether. He intended to incapacitate her using the ether. The jurors also viewed the tire poppers. Other factors regarding the heinousness of his crimes came into play. There were elements of torture, Anderson took Piper right in front of her children, and he made his deviant plans over months and years. The jurors listened intently.

When the testimony concluded, the jury silently filed out of the room. The tension became unbearable until once again, everyone was called in to hear the verdict. The jurors were polled individually to verbalize their decision. One by one, all came back with the same announcement. Anderson would be put to death. Robert Leroy Anderson showed no pity for his victims, and the jury in turn showed no pity for him. He would face the executioner's needle.

As a sadistic killer, Anderson blossomed and honed his crimes at a young age. He fell out of the norm. Statistics indicate that the type of murders Anderson carried out are generally done by older perpetrators, mid- to late thirties up to late forties. He became a deviant and acted on it in an aggressive manner. The prosecution's success nailed one of the most horrific criminals to have ever terrorized the tri-state area.

The former homecoming queen, Piper Streyle, was abducted from her home in broad daylight.

Larisa and Bill Dumansky, along with their two daughters, escaped religious persecution in the Ukraine and came to America for the promise of a better life.

The day before Piper was abducted, Nathan turned two years old and received the blue play tent as a birthday present. The whole family climbed inside for a special photo.

Robert Anderson profiled beautiful young women and Amy Anderson (no relation to Robert) caught his eye.

The jury was able to view one of the tire-poppers during the penalty phase of the murder trial.

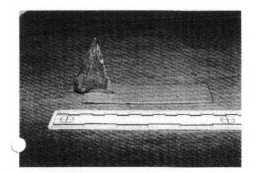

The Bronco was a treasure-trove of criminal evidence.

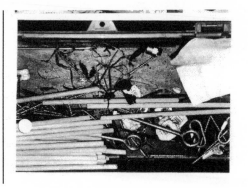

A toolbox in the back of the Bronco contained items of a heinous nature. Investigators referred to it as "the torture kit."

The "bondage board," with eye rings in the corners, was designed to fit in the back of the Bronco.

The mystery of the rectangular silhouettes on the bondage board came to light when prosecutor Larry Long discovered that a tire-popper fit exactly inside the shape. Anderson spray-painted these devices various colors so they would be difficult to detect on a dark road.

Half of Piper's nightshirt was discovered in Anderson's secret crime location.

When a citizen discovered half of the nightshirt lying on a road, he had no idea of the significance of his discovery and intended to use it as a rag to clean his car.

Sheriff Gene Taylor was the first to arrive at the Streyle residence after Piper's disappearance. His wife, Lois, and family were actively involved in the search for the young mother.

Special Agent Bob Grandpre's extensive experience interviewing sex offenders became vital when questioning Anderson for the first time.

DCI Agent Jim Severson was integral in investigating the case against Anderson. Severson has still not given up the search for Piper's body.

Anderson's bizarre sexual desires were fueled by bondage pornography. He made elaborate plans to abduct, rape, and murder women.

The cunning inmate Jeremy Brunner was able to gain the trust of Anderson and elicit vital information about the murders. Brunner's efforts helped the prosecution land a death sentence for Anderson.

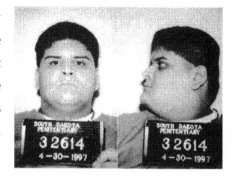

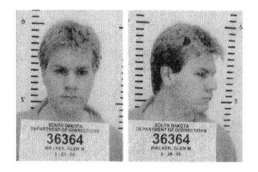

Anderson's longtime friend Glen Walker became an accomplice.

Walker Walks the Walks

AS THE HAMMER was falling on Anderson, Glen Walker tried to sidestep justice by cooperating with authorities. It was too late. He had left the telephone recording message about trying to help Anderson with an alibi. Then he provided information about Larisa's grave without making a deal for immunity. This turned into a web of confusion with Walker claiming he thought he had a plea deal and the state's attorney remaining adamant that although Walker offered to plead guilty to a misdemeanor charge of not reporting a crime, the offer was never accepted. Walker's attempt to float under the radar for his part in the heinous crimes ended with Walker facing his own set of charges. The State hit him with Conspiracy to Commit Kidnapping of Larisa Dumansky, Kidnapping and Murder of Larisa Dumansky, Conspiracy to Commit Kidnapping and Murder of Amy Anderson, Attempted Kidnapping and Attempted Murder of Amy Anderson, an Alternate count of Conspiring to Commit Kidnapping and Murder. Walker was indicted on August 18, 1998, and arrested within a week. He was considered an accessory to the Streyle case due to leaving the tape-recorded false alibi.

In a strange twist, a television station re-aired footage of the search for Piper Streyle that had occurred immediately after her disappearance. Coincidentally, someone noticed that Glen Walker was one of the searchers in the news clip. His bizarre connections to the crimes fueled the prosecutors to make sure he would be held accountable for his involvements. Investigators speculated he joined the search to keep tabs on whether anyone suspected something amiss with the chokecherry bush.

Jeremy Brunner's testimony would contain the most important evidence against Walker. Both sides knew this. In a series of legal battles that went all the way to the State Supreme Court, the defense fought desperately to exclude Brunner's testimony while the prosecution fought equally hard to allow the jury to hear him. After eight months of appeals, it was ruled that Brunner could not testify against Walker. This was primarily because Brunner never spoke directly with Walker the way he had with Anderson. Without Brunner, the prosecution could not place Walker at Larisa's kidnapping or the attempted kidnapping of Amy Anderson. The loss was a serious blow to the state.

"After considering the new hand we were dealt, we determined there was a definite risk that Walker could be acquitted," Long explained. So the prosecution offered a plea agreement. There was enough evidence that Walker faced life in prison if he went to trial and lost. This made him nervous enough that he did not want to face a criminal trial. Through his lawyers, Walker went for the plea agreement.

The agreement included a "clear out," meaning that Walker had to tell every small detail he knew about the crimes. In exchange, he would receive a 25-year sentence and would get transactional immunity, which meant he could not be charged with any other crime related to Dumansky, Streyle, or Amy Anderson. To determine whether he was telling the truth, he had to take a polygraph test, and if he failed, another five years would be added to his sentence. There were high hopes that the clear out would provide information about the location of Piper's body.

Walker revealed that about two weeks prior to Larisa's abduction, Anderson had taken him to the Morrell's parking lot and described how he would carry out the kidnapping. There were more small details about the crimes but nothing critical and nothing about the whereabouts of Piper. When Walker finished with the clear out, he was given a polygraph that lasted over two hours. Walker failed. Two of his answers indicated deception: *Did you kill Larisa Dumansky the night of her disappearance? Did you have sexual intercourse with her?*

Walker felt guilty and was under extreme stress, his defense lawyers countered. Besides, they considered the examiner to be incompetent. A second polygraph test with a different examiner was scheduled. When asked three of the questions, "Did you witness the death of Larisa?" "Have you misstated any information about Larisa's death?" and "Did you have sexual contact with Larisa?" Walker answered "No" to all of them. The examiner determined that Walker did not respond truthfully.

Again, the defense blamed the failed polygraph test on Walker being emotionally devastated. They pointed out that when Anderson spilled his story to Brunner behind bars, Anderson was mad at Walker and had no reason to minimize his former friend's involvement. Yet, he never mentioned Walker doing anything other than that to which Walker admitted. The judge didn't buy it and added five years onto Walker's sentence, adding that he reserved his sympathy for the victims and their families.

He received a 30-year sentence, making him eligible for parole after 14 years. Bill Dumansky was simply glad the case was over, and although he believed Walker was sincerely sorry, it was too late. The 14 years Walker would likely serve was nothing compared to the years Larisa lost with her children and family.

Walker was denied parole each time he became eligible, but due to good behavior, he served about half of his sentence and was released on Christmas Eve in 2015. Upon his release, there were no restrictions of parole or probation guidelines to follow. Ultimately, Walker left South Dakota, but the terror he helped to create remained. The crimes were a life sentence of fear for so many people who will forever live with the lingering memories and were a death sentence for Larisa and Piper.

Brunner

JEREMY BRUNNER SERVED his time in the South Dakota Penitentiary and rode off into the criminal sunset. He left the state, and those in law enforcement familiar with Brunner lost track of him. Long commented, "Jeremy Brunner may end up spending eternity in hell, but the guy sure deserves some good conduct medals for his role in bringing to justice the murderer of two innocent women, an unborn baby, and others Anderson victimized."

Like Father, Like Son

ANDERSON EXISTED IN his 6x13-foot cell painted a drab green that supposedly had a calming effect on the inmates. He stayed in the ad seg wing eating up taxpayer dollars. To avoid the executioner's needle, his attorney filed the necessary appeals which left Anderson with the mundane life of lockdown 23 hours each day, Monday through Friday. He was allowed out of his cell for a forty-five-minute exercise period and shower, but weekends were twenty-four-hour lockdown. He was not allowed a cellmate or exercise partner. With a Class 2 visitation policy, he talked via phone through thick glass with an occasional family member as a visitor. His wife, Elaine, said she had to move on with her life and divorced him. When his sickening crimes were exposed, past friends and acquaintances wanted nothing to do with him as well.

In December of 2002, Anderson's father, who lived near Yankton, South Dakota, put a gun to his head and ended his life. Anderson had long experienced a complicated relationship with his troubled father. He masked the impact of the death, although guards noticed a change in his demeanor. Control was Anderson's oxygen. He had to have it and began a plan. The biggest obstacle to his plan was limited access to contraband. Prison staff often pondered the mystery of how certain illegal items made their way into a cell. The expanded security of death row increased the difficulty for a con to get contraband. In March of 2003, during a random shakedown of cells and only a few months after Leland committed suicide, guards discovered a razor blade hidden under the inner edge of Anderson's small table. He was shackled and moved into an isolation cell due to the rule violation and to give the prison authorities time to investigate the incident to see if Anderson intended to harm himself.

In the isolation area, Anderson was checked on every fifteen minutes. The sound of shoes coming down the shiny waxed corridor announced the routine check was coming. The correctional officer paused at Anderson's cell and, as required, made eye contact with the convict, who was sitting on the side of his bed. As soon as the footsteps faded to the end of the tier, Anderson hopped up and quickly went to work. He tightly knotted an end of his bed sheet to a cross bar on the cell door, then slipped the other end of the sheet he had fashioned into a noose around his neck. Letting his body become dead weight, he hung from the cell door, without ever admitting guilt or revealing the location of Piper. Her final resting place was possibly lost forever.

Fifteen minutes later, a guard found Anderson with a bluish discolored face and his tongue swollen and protruding. He shouted for more correctional officers, and two prison nurses also came sprinting to assist. They cut Anderson down and immediately began CPR. He had no pulse or respiration. The nurses positioned a defibrillator, and his body jerked with the first surge of electricity. The life-saving techniques continued until an ambulance transported him to a local hospital, where he was pronounced dead. Newspaper headlines reported Anderson's suicide to the satisfaction of many who had followed the case.

Vance commented, "My life will not be altered by what he chose to do to himself."

Long possibly summed up best the sentiments of the community when he said, "A lot of women will rest better tonight knowing Robert Leroy Anderson is no longer around."

***

FOLLOWING THE MURDER trial and Anderson's suicide, unanswered questions lingered. The killer shared private information with Brunner but obviously kept some of his dark secrets to himself. Though he never explained his actions, it was theorized he used the vibrator and candle to torture Piper before he murdered her. The purpose of the red yarn found in the Bronco was never determined. On the night Amy Anderson was nearly abducted on the dark highway, investigators discussed two theories. One is that Robert Anderson and Walker stalked and possibly followed the women that night waiting for the right opportunity. Another theory is that it was a combination of coincidence and bad luck. Amy and her friend happened to travel down the same road where Anderson and Walker were trolling for victims.

***

BLACK SMOKE BILLOWED skyward. In a pit of earth, the bondage board crackled and then burst into flames, surrounded by a pile of items last seen on the evidence table of a courtroom. Following Anderson's suicide, there would be no more appeals. The attorney general filed paperwork to destroy the physical evidence from the trials. DCI Agent Severson and Paulette Petersen from the crime lab were given the task of destroying the evidence. The Bronco was stored at the state crime lab in Pierre, South Dakota; Severson and Petersen made arrangements for it to be crushed. Then they went to the McCook County Courthouse, where a dump truck backed up to the old jail, an area now used to house trial evidence due to its secure location. Severson had a complete list of evidence and checked items off the list as they were tossed into the truck. At the county landfill, they doused the pile with gasoline and tossed in a match. Severson couldn't help but feel that some of the evil disappeared with the rising smoke.

All of the investigators, volunteers, prayers, and tears couldn't bring Piper home. With Anderson's death went all hope of him revealing the location of her remains. No part of Piper has ever been located except for the head hairs found on the board and duct tape. For Sheriff Taylor, the crimes still haunt him. "You want so badly to find her, and when you don't, it stays with you." Taylor considers Anderson the closest thing to Satan he has ever encountered.

Severson still can't let go. "These crimes affected me in a way no other case has. Anderson told Brunner that Piper was put in the river of a back cove and beneath a log jam. We searched heavily and never found an area of the river that fit that description. I have always felt that Anderson buried Piper somewhere in the blue play tent. Sexual sadists like Anderson need the souvenirs of their crimes: jewelry, a purse, clothing, or something so that they can relive the excitement of their deeds. We know Anderson visited Larisa Dumansky's gravesite several times, and I think he buried Piper so that he could return to her also. Until I take my last breath on this Earth, I won't give up trying to find Piper," he explained.

A few years back, Severson received information about a location that might hold Piper's remains. He obtained a search warrant and dug up the site. The tip was another letdown in the search for Piper, but he refuses to give up hope that someday she will be returned to her family.

***

WITH A CAREER in the judicial system that spanned forty-five years, Long reflected on the multitudes of people he encountered. "Most people who have broken laws come into the courtroom and have behaviors that can be explained. They may have become hooked on gambling, drugs, or alcohol, suffer from PTSD, or have momentarily lost their temper. But Robert Anderson was plain evil. He didn't commit any of his crimes while on drugs or alcohol, and he spent months planning while stone-cold sober. He carried out his terrible deeds because he loved it, and part of his joy was reliving the crimes. Thank God our world doesn't have many Robert Andersons."

Do not be overcome by evil, but overcome evil with good.

—Romans 12:21

Postscript

The dark cloud of Anderson's hideous crimes lingered. It led to the inevitable question of *how can God allow such things to happen?* People who hold Christian beliefs feel God did not allow it to happen. Satan is the creator of evil and misery; he is the reason we have suffering and death. The powers of evil win many battles on Earth. Robert Anderson chose to use his hands and mind as instruments of Satan, but in the end, God and goodness will win the war even though many battles will be lost along the way. God has rescued his people from death through His son, Jesus. Regardless of religious beliefs, many saw the tragedies as shedding light on the need for better mental health programs and ways to identify children with emotional problems before they develop into a Robert Leroy Anderson. Vance shared a reflective moment with Long when he said he felt that Piper lost her life but in doing so saved other women from a similar fate. Because of Piper, Anderson was finally arrested.

John and Jean Potts returned to Texas after expressing some final thoughts. "It's nice to know that your child has reconciled to God," John said. "If we had no hope, it would be harder. This is not the end. It's an interruption…a brutal one, but we'll see her again."

When Larisa and Piper left this world, they left their children in good hands. Instead of allowing the tragedy of the crimes to consume them, Bill and Vance, with extraordinary courage, did just the opposite. Keeping God as a guiding light, they raised their children to become loving and successful adults. The darkness that descended on their childhoods could not extinguish the light of their faith. The Dumansky and Streyle children continue to experience lives filled with love, compassion, adventure, and community service. The children have climbed mountains, walked in the ocean waves, visited foreign countries, earned college degrees, and surrounded themselves with friends and children. Their family photos are rich with smiles. They keep love at the forefront of their lives. It has been said that being loved gives strength while loving others gives meaning and courage. It's this powerful emotion that continues to sustain them.

Bill and Vance also rebuilt their personal lives with happiness. Both remarried. But the cherished memories of days gone by remain. Vance said, "I loved Piper, and I still do love her. I thank God for her touching my life and with earnest expectation know that I will see her again in eternity."

PHIL AND SANDY HAMMAN are the authors of *Gitchie Girl* and *Gitchie Girl Uncovered,* both national bestsellers in true crime. The Hammans also co-authored *Rap Sheet* after Phil penned his memoirs *Under the Influence* and *disOrder.* They have been married since 1984 and reside in northwest Iowa. Both are longtime public-school educators. They have been blessed with two children and four grandchildren. Phil and Sandy enjoy spending time writing in quiet seclusion in their cabin overlooking an expansive river valley.

LARRY LONG is a lifelong resident of South Dakota. During his prestigious 45-year career, he was an attorney, State's Attorney for Bennett County, and Chief Deputy to the South Dakota Attorney General before being elected to two terms as South Dakota Attorney General. He was appointed Circuit Court judge in 2009 and retired in 2018. Larry earned several awards including the Region II Trial Lawyer of the Year in 1999. He created the Open Government Task Force, a statewide Cold Case Investigation Unit, and the 24/7 Sobriety Project. He and his wife, Jan, have two children and two grandchildren.

Made in the USA
Monee, IL
04 February 2021